THE Z FILES

TREASURES FROM ZACHERLEY'S ARCHIVES

BY

RICHARD SCRIVANI

WITH TOM WEAVER

On the cover: In a posed shot from his WOR show, Zacherley the Cool Ghoul reads the book *Transylvania: The Land Beyond the Forest* by Louis C. Cornish.

The Z Files: Treasures From Zacherley's Archives
© 2012 Richard Scrivani. All Rights Reserved.

Published in the USA by:
BearManor Media
PO Box 1129
Duncan, Oklahoma 73534-1129
www.bearmanormedia.com

ISBN 978-1-59393-XXX-X

Printed in the United States of America.
Cover design by Kerry Gammill.
Book design by Brian Pearce | Red Jacket Press.

TABLE OF CONTENTS

Dedicated to The Duck

John Zacherle and the author in 2009.

INTRODUCTION

In 2004, John Zacherle and I were in his Manhattan apartment, exploring and cleaning out the Legendary Zacherley Closet, looking for memorabilia that we could photograph and feature on the upcoming DVD documentary *The Zacherley Archives*. We came upon a large cardboard box packed with items I had been hoping — but not really expecting — to find. There before my eyes was a large cache of newspaper clippings, yellowed and fragile. In my Monster Kid imagination, it was not unlike unearthing an urn of tana leaves. Did we dare leaf through them, or would they disappear in a snowstorm of confetti, like the row of ancient books discovered in the Eloi library by Rod Taylor in *The Time Machine*?

Also in the Closet were various pieces of artwork and other mementos that Zach had received back in the late 1950s from his more creative fans. Digging yet further, we turned up a small collection of handwritten notes and typed scripts from those important years in the Zacherley-Roland history. The articles and scripts didn't seem to be appropriate for the *Zacherley Archives* DVD bonus feature "Zach's Closet," so back in the closet they went. That's where they remained until I realized that these treasures, not seen for nearly 50 years, should be preserved between two book covers for all Zacherley fans to enjoy.

Hence the birth of the idea for the book you are now holding in your misshapen mitts. But work did not begin in earnest until a few years later. When Zach gave me unlimited access to his "files," I started carefully sifting through piles of articles and publicity material, contracts, and in one case even a Zacherle-typed journal chronicling his circuitous journey from Philadelphia fame as TV host "Roland" to a final deal in New York as "Zacherley."

I summarized that sequence of events in my first book *Good Night, Whatever You Are!* (2006) but now interested fans can see the documents themselves and read step-by-step what it took (and took *away* from) Zach to finally set up his crypt in the Big Apple.

At various points in this book Zach himself adds his comments, shedding a bit more light on certain phases of his career. You will also be treated to a host of photos, many never before published, thanks to the generosity of the Cool Ghoul.

The Z Files could never have come to fruition without the hard work of my Monster Kid colleague Tom Weaver, who brought his experience, encouragement — and his lightning-fast typing skills — to the project. Additional thanks and appreciation to Marty Baumann, John and Ruth Brunas, Michael Brunas, Kevin Clement, Arnie DeGaetano, Rosemary DiPietra, Christine Domaniecki, Kerry Gammill, Michael and Ruth Gilks, Barry Landers, Joette Hampton-Martin, John Morgan, George Ann Muller, Paul Russak, Jeff Samuels, Paul Scrabo, Michael R. Thomas, Terry Tousey and…John Zacherle.

Rich Scrivani
April 2012

1

JOHN ZACHERLE
THE EARLY YEARS

COME WITH ME TO PENNSYLVANIA
JOHN ZACHERLE RECALLS HIS EARLY LIFE

Growing up in the Philadelphia area was kinda neat. Our house had a great park behind it and a semi-pro baseball team that used to "pass the hat" after their games. There was a quarry beside us until the guy who owned it decided to turn it into a playground. It became a really great community place: a huge sandbox with a big building over it, open on all sides, about as big as a merry-go-round carousel structure. They had seesaws all over the place and swings. We used to climb around what was left of the quarry, and it wasn't a hard rock, it was kind of crumbly. Whenever we were spotted, they would send somebody to chase us for fear we'd be injured.

It was great because there were a lot of kids there, most of them several years older than my friend Charlie Levy and me. Charlie's mother called him "Snooky," so we called him that. Charlie had an older brother, Richard, who my brother hung out with. My cousins lived nearby and there was another wonderful park about two blocks in the other direction called Fern Hill where we'd go skiing and sledding. They also played baseball up there, the same teams. Our home team was the Happy Hollow White Sox. That big park is still there, next to an industrial area with a steel works where Budd Manufacturing made railroad cars. Every once in a while there would be this terrifying noise or a whistle, meaning there'd been an accident at the plant. It was a very ominous thing to hear it going off. There was also a big reservoir, and the other side of it was where Grace Kelly lived with her family. Near the river there was a whole stretch of boathouses where guys would go rowing in sculls — that's where Grace Kelly's brother Jack hung out. For years we'd go down and watch the boat races with all the colleges rowing. That was a great event, to go there and sit and have a picnic and look down the hill at the Schuylkill River. It was like being in the top seat of a double-decker stadium. They used to have the trolley cars, the summer trolleys and winter trolleys that went through the park. They never should have gotten rid of them. They'd be a great attraction now.

We had a movie house right next to the playground. We only saw family movies, of course. When talkies came in, at first they had the sound on a big disc, not on the film. The voices would get way out of sync, and the projectionist would have to move the needle or something. We in the audience had to make a lot of noise clapping or stomping if it went out of sync and the projectionist wasn't paying attention. I was never allowed to see horror films.

Saturday evening sometimes we'd go off in groups, hiking up into the area where the big theaters were. We had two very large ones, with balconies, one with a great, sweeping auditorium where we could get a good view from any seat. They're all gone now. My parents liked Sigmund Romberg and stuff like that. One of my father's favorites was John Philip Sousa.

Everybody got along fine in our family. My sister had her own room. My oldest brother was eight years older so he and the middle brother shared the biggest room in the back of the house. My mother and father's room was in the front. I had a tiny room because I was a tiny kid! At some point, probably just before the war, we moved from Germantown to Chestnut Hill. My sister told me I should go see some lady in charge of hiring summer help at the Providence Trust Co., which was run by Quakers. I was really no good at office work. I just didn't like concentrating and I had to keep track of various businesses' accounts, and I could never get it right. Every day a nice young guy would come over and try to straighten me out. I was not too hot at that business. I think my father wanted everybody to have some kind of profession and I don't think they knew what to do with me.

So I tried acting...

ABOVE: *A 2008 shot of Zach in front of his childhood home in Germantown PA.* BELOW: *A 2008 photo of the playground used by Zach and his friends in the late 1920s.*

DING EAGLE, WEDNESDAY, AUGUST 11, 1954

Berks Players Score Hit With 'My Three Angels'

The Berks Players have reached a new high in summer theater with their production of "My Three Angels," a superbly acted, directed and staged play now being shown at the Green Hills Theater.

The play features the highly imaginative acting of a tried and true cast of actors, headed by the incomparable Joseph Gistirak and featuring a newcomer to the company, John Zacherle, Philadelphia.

Gistirak, now in his sixth role with the Berks Players, never turned in a more interesting performance. His acting is quick and precise, reflecting a talent perfectly at home in the various roles he has enacted. In none of them, however, has he been comparable to his role as "Joseph," the convict, in "My Three Angels."

Zacherle's introspective acting is a treat, displaying, as it does, a quality seldom found in any except the most intense of profes-

sional thespians. His interpretation of "Papa Jules," the second convict, is one of the warmest roles enacted on the Green Hills stage. Watching him, one seems to see the whole process enacted before one's eyes: The idea, the conflict it creates, the solution (if there is one) suggested, the action that naturally follows from it. What a joy to watch such acting!

William Schou, the third convict and the third of "the three angels," made his most interesting appearance of the season as "Alfred," a young man doomed to promoting for someone else what he himself can never have—perfect happiness.

April Night, who made her debut with the Berks Players in "Lysistrata," also brought new life to her acting in "My Three Angels." Miss Night is pert and

winsome, and with more substantial roles might carve for herself the place she undoubtedly wants in the theater.

Fran Stridinger made a handsome and attractive "Emilie Ducotel," but other roles have given her better opportunity to show her talents. She was hardly more convincing as the colonial storekeeper's wife than Ken Chapin was as "Felix Ducotel," the storekeeper.

Other company favorites, including Charles Schulte and Carl Wagner, respectively as "Henri and Paul Trochard," enlivened the fast-moving comedy. The cast also includes Irma Lee Hurley and Robert Morris.

"My Three Angels," as a play, is one of the best choices to have been made by Director Mesrop Kesdekian. It was written by Sam and Bella Spewack from Albert Husson's "La Cuisine de Anges," and is set in Cayenne, French Guiana. The play concerns the Ducotel family at Christmas, 1910.

How the three convicts sent by providence as three angels work out the difficulties facing the family Ducotel makes one of the brightest and funniest evenings of theater presented here.

It gets our vote as the best play of the season, and one that will be remembered locally long after "Lysistra" and "Gigi" have faded from memory.—L.P.H.

Don't Let

Zach made his Berks Players debut in their 1954 production My Three Angels. *Zach says, "At this theater [the Green Hills Theater], each show ran just one or two weeks.* My Three Angels *took place in the Caribbean, where the French owned land at the time. They used to send all their prisoners there. I played one of the prisoners, a very mild-mannered guy, not a murderer or anything like that."* FAR RIGHT: *A review of Zach's second Berks Players production,* Dear Brutus.

Play Continues a Week

John Zacherle is shown here in his role as one of the convicts in "My Three Angels," the Berks Players' production that will continue each weekday evening this week at 8:30 o'clock in the Green Hills Theater, Morgantown Road. William Schou and Joseph Gistirak also portray convicts. The trio aids a family in French Guiana.

REA.

'Dear Brutus' Pleases Opening Night Audience at Green Hills

The combination of deft acting, an incredibly beautiful set and intelligent directing has fashioned "Dear Brutus" into one of the most interesting productions yet staged by the Berks Players at the Green Hills Theater.

The play, written by Sir James M. Barrie, opened a week-long run last night, and to the audience who viewed it on opening night it seemed to be studded with delights.

The mystery that shrouds Lob, portrayed by young Ronald Suny, and his odd house guests, gathered in a peculiar old house between the moor, the mountains and the sea, builds almost from the moment the curtain rises on the set John Lear designed for the production.

Often hailed as a comedy, "Dear Brutus" is also a drama, filled with pathos and wishfulness. It is, in short, a fantasy, tender and touching in the subtle shadowing of the characters, real and unreal, whom Barrie presents.

The action centers around Lob, also known as Puck, and the house guests, of whom all but one have a wish in common — to have a second chance in life.

How each of them gets that opportunity makes one of the most delightful evenings of theater the Berks Players have done. With such a beautiful play available, it is curious that no other local theater group has ever presented it.

With so large a cast, and so many of them cast in roles of equal might, it is difficult to single out one or two as being superlative. It's not difficult, however, to see and admit that every member of the cast was working at top speed, giving the best of which he was capable.

Mildred Ice has never given a better performance than in her roel as Mrs. Purdie, nor Charles Schulte as the wastrel artist who is her husband. Irma Lee Hurley, as the artist's "never was" daughter, gave one of the most spar-

kling performances of the evening.

John Zacherle, who made his acting debut with the players two weeks ago in "My Three Angels," was superb. But so were Ken Chapin, William Schou, Ronald Suny, Fran Stridinger, Irma Cohen, the only one of the guests who does not seek a second chance; Pat Hale and April Night.

Mesrop Kesdekian directed the play, and achieved a superb job of interpreting and fitting together a difficult piece of theater.

Not only is Lear's set stunning — it almost steals the opening scene from the actors — but it also is ingenious to a marvelous degree. The set was constructed by Ted Moore. The change from Lob's house to the magic wood at the end of the first act is just about the cleverest bit of stagecraft the Berks Players have brought off in three summers at Green Hills.

"Dear Brutus" is one of their finest!—L.P.H.

ZACH: *"Before I did television, I was trying to figure out what to do with my life and somebody got me to go downtown [Philadelphia] and be in still pictures for magazines."*

2
ROLAND

BY THE WINTER OF 1957, THOUSANDS OF AMERICANS WERE CAPTIVATED BY LATE-NIGHT MONSTER MOVIES THANKS TO SCREEN GEMS' "SHOCK!," A PACKAGE OF VINTAGE MOVIES RELEASED TO LOCAL STATIONS NATIONWIDE. MANY MAJOR CITIES ENHANCED THE CELLULOID CHILLS WITH THE ADDITION OF A HOST WHO GUIDED WIDE-EYED WATCHERS THROUGH THIS WEIRD WORLD OF WEREWOLVES, MUMMIES, MAD SCIENTISTS AND WORSE. ON CHANNEL 10 IN PHILADELPHIA, THAT HOST WAS JOHN ZACHERLE'S ROLAND.

Lehigh Valley Radio-TV Shopper, Allentown, Pa. 1-23-58

Roland—Shock Theatre Specialist

John Zacherle, more popularly known as Roland of WCAU-TV's "Shock Theatre," and his show writer, Ed White, have much fun on the job . . . while thinking up new ideas for the "Shock Theatre" introductions, they take time out to look over some of the many objects which have been sent to Roland by his admirers. 12,000 pieces of mail were received in just one week after Roland asked his viewers to send him 3 hairs from their head in order that he might make a "human" pillow for his wife.

Included in the varied list of fantastic articles which Roland has received since his "Shock Theatre" debut last fall are: a preserved heart (animal), 2 pints of human blood, a brain (animal) in a box, several "bloody" mailmen's whistles, a freshly skinned antelope head, 2 animal skulls, a shrunken head in a coffin, a pair of "hands" in a coffin, 2 hangman's nooses, several pairs of cuff links, with weird designs such as skulls, scorpions, etc., a carrot, sculptured in the shape of a corpse, reclining in a casket, and dozens of handkerchiefs embroidered with appropriate "Shock Theatre" designs.

Roland's gifts are sent to him in the same vein in which he presents his show each Monday and Tuesday at 11:25 PM on Channel 10 . . . gruesome at times, yes, but in a light-hearted, tongue-in-cheek manner.

For instance, he's gotten 5 plaster-of-paris death masks; several "voodo" dolls, a pair of earrings from the "Werewolf which was running loose in South Philadelphia," box of chocolate-covered ants, a can of caterpillars, keys dripping (catsup) blood, a model "bloodnik," a skull salt and pepper set resting on a china casket.

In addition to his regular mail containing thousands of cards and letters, Roland's collection includes telegrams, poetry, and numerous pieces of art work . . . some 20 portraits of Roland, conceptions of what his mysterious sidekick and his wife in the casket look like.

Early in Zach's TV career, he played an undertaker on Action in the Afternoon *(1953-54), a live Western running on Philly's WCAU Channel 10. A few years later, he received a call from WCAU president Charlie Vanda, who remembered him as the undertaker and offered him the chance to play a new character created by producer Ed White: Roland, the ghoulish host of* The Shock Theatre.

HORROR HOST Roland, in real life John Zacherle, a longtime Germantown resident, gets ready to give viewers on WCAU-TV a full evening of shock and fun.

'Roland Once 'Haunted' Streets Of Germantown

By PAUL CATHEY

As the midnight hour approaches most residents in The Courier area are settling down at home.

One, however, is still hard at work. And what ghoulish work it is! Supposedly deep in the earth (but really in a WCAU-TV studio) a dour fiend named Roland (pronounced Ro-lan) is cavorting. Roland, otherwise actor John Zacherle, a longtime Germantown resident, is a sort of other-world master of ceremonies.

He was created last October when the station wanted a "live" host on its late at night screenings of horror movies. So now Roland, together with his camera-shy, man Friday, Igor, presides over the WCAU-TV Shock Theatre every Friday and Saturday at 11:25 p.m.

Roland does it from his TV "home," set up to resemble a subterranean crypt complete with chains, a hangman's noose, candles and casket. In residence in the casket is "My Dear," presumably Mrs. Roland. (Neither Igor or My Dear are ever seen, but through dialogue, sound effects, and action they

When Roland offered his picture to anyone sending in three human hairs, the station got over 18,000 pieces of mail, including one IOU from a baldheaded man.

Germantown Graduate

With the show's popularity Zacherle has gotten used to being recognized as Roland even while away from the studio and without makeup. The 39-year-old actor, a graduate of Germantown High and the University of Pennsylvania, has done the part since its beginning last October. And that's more than 50 appearances as Roland.

In pre-Roland days several years ago he took part in WCAU's outdoor live TV western, "Action in the Afternoon," appearing as an old prospector and an undertaker. Courier readers may remember him in the parts he played with the Stagecrafters of Chestnut Hill in the years between 1949 and 1955.

Recently Zacherle made a recording in the macabre manner. It's a double sider, called Dinner With Drac, Part I and Part II. The record is a recitation of ghoulish verses with background be-bop

parties. He's been showered with fan mail with many writers wanting to form fan clubs. A fantastic assortment of "gifts"—including a miniature casket and a sequinned bat—have poured in from listeners.

When Zacherle as Roland showed up for a personal appearance at an Allentown automotive dealer's, the showroom got so crowded he had to make an "escape" through an auto wash rack trap door.

But it's not always that hectic. On those occasions when Roland isn't around you'll find actor Zacherle working around his garden or tinkering with his 1941 Buick.

After all, even a "ghoul" deserves some time off.

See in person-"alive" ROLAND

STAR of "SHOCK THEATRE"
CHANNEL 10

See Roland in his first public appearance anywhere, except Transylvania of course.

ABOVE: *Newspaper ad announcing Roland's first-ever public appearance (a January 17, 1958, sales event at Town Auto Chevrolet on Hanover Avenue in Allentown PA).*

FLOURTOWN'S SHOCK THEATRE

Roland, famed sleep-wrecker and No. 1 spook on WCAU-TV's Shock Theatre, is John Zackerle, of Flourtown and member of the Stagecrafters. A bachelor, he's got all the girls scared to death.

By BETTY BROD

Follow-up on Roland. He of the late Horror Show on WCAU-TV. Late—meaning time of night—his wife being really the "late" MY DEAR. Roland does the commercials—but has become much more important than any of the vintage movies his sponsors make him introduce.

Well, Roland "let drop", one night last week,, that he would be having "Open House" at WCAU on City Avenue, Saturday afternoon, and we had a bid to go and pay our respects. Advance scuttlebutt had it that only the college crowd and spoprts car set would be at all interested in taking the time to say hello—but how wrong can you get?

Grandparents dragging five year olds were there; middle aged females; teenagers—PEOPLE!! Over (an estimated) fourteen thousand of them. The reception was called for one o'clock. By 10:30 a.m., the powers that be decided to open one half hour earlier, because the mob was getting too big. Traffic was tied up for blocks around the building, and City Line Bridge was solid with cars.

The grounds around the TV station were being trampled to a sea of mud by the hundreds of people queued up to get into the building. Philadelphia police and Merion Township Police had their hands full. Announcements kept coming over the radio — the police were trying to re-route traffic around the area, and who got in to see Roland? Quite a few; the patient, and the early birds. One of the highlights? was the sight of four boys, one made up to resemble Roland, carrying a coffin.

THE PHILADELPHIA INQUIRER, THURSDAY

rms
en,
ir

les and
out of
ween.
e of the
said in
sipping a

prices in
one wants
s TV show
rify view-
quite flat-
g when
stop to
about

loff, who
won a
ful baby
st, has
l to his
cing de-
nor by
wing a
gly white
rd. Con-
hy skin,
onvulsive
s enough
cret po-

Scre
Ph

By I
The part
phia polic
wholesale I
addicts and
"Armstrong
an engrossin
   Although in
melodramati
ing a nick-of-
Marines resc
of baddies w
rookie policew
demanding she
licly that she v
professed to I
Junkie's Alley'
ring of authentic
   This was bolst
preparations for
the appearance,
hour, of two ac
Philadelphia's fi
ine A. Kelley, h
policewomen, a
McDermott, chie
tectives.
   Monica Lovett v
traught as Police
who accepted her r
assignment despi
qualms, and Bert
plenty of menace
net's prize catch.
         * *
L AST night's
      Secret" was a f
several ways. G

Halloween-style characters have been making nonholiday appearances in connection with a TV series of old horror movies. In New York, spooky honors were performed by a vampire (left); in Hollywood, by a hair-on-end "Miss Nightmare." In Philadelphia, the "Shock" films are hosted by the eerie Roland.

Roland, Igor Bring Out 'Beast' in Roddy Hall Men

By ROYCE WALTERS

If you hear the cry of a wolf, don't be alarmed; it's the mark of a disciple of Roland, the latest campus fad. Roland, the congenial host of Shock Theater, is seen from 11:25 p.m. to 1 a.m. on Monday and Tuesday nights on WCAU-TV, Channel 10.

Roland's diabolical humor has packed to capacity the canteens of Roddy Hall and Old Main dormitories. In fact, some men start watching TV at 9 o'clock to be sure they have a good seat for the show. There have been some complaints from the girls who, having to be in their rooms at that time, can't hear Roland's wit and repartee.

Get Real Shock

Consternation and feelings of dismay ran high in Roddy Hall last Monday night since some mischievous little muskrat chewed through the lead-in cable and disrupted the TV service. However, on Tuesday night the faithful fans assembled to see and hear Roland and his pet beast, the faithful, invisible, always growling Igor.

Campus notables such as Jerry Pasternak, Stan Stout, Tom Carver and Jack Spiese have made Shock Theater their "life's concern." They wouldn't dream of missing a show; moreover, it's even spreading to the faculty.

Roland uses the most fascinating props. Over his desk — that is, the casket whose lid is always sliding around — he narrates the show. Sometimes during the show Roland can't resist and climbs into the casket which houses the corpse of his sweetheart to show his affection for her. Of course, there are the more usual props like shrunken heads, withered hands, plenty of blood, too, all at the perfect temperature of 98.6 degrees.

Watch for Host

Some of the movies feature Dracula, Frankenstein, The Vampire and Wolfman. I might add the show is watched not so much to see the movies, but to see the host, the maniacal Roland.

Some of the more faithful followers sleep and finish all homework during the day just so they're free to watch Roland. The men in the dorms are very enthusiastic about the program and as you walk through the halls you hear the calls of Igor, Roland, and other weird noises associated with the show.

And as Roland says, "Goodnight, whatever you are."

"THE SNAPPER"
MILLERSVILLE, PA. NOV. 13, 1957

THE VILLANOVAN   December 11, 1957

PUBlicly Speaking

Roland Amuses TV Viewers

By MIKE KLESIUS

To my understanding, there is a certain late television show receiving a great deal of attention. Roland (Roe-lun) seems to have worked wonders on the campus residents. His sadistic and crude methods of displaying horror have won the hearts of every possible viewer between the hours of eleven-thirty and one o'clock. Roland at the beginning of his "Shock Theatre" was the butt of every rude remark that the viewing audience could muster together. But since then, this pitiful looking creature has become a rather fashionable laughing point.

Pouring red liquids back and forth, rattling chains, slamming doors, and most of all lingering over odd shapes under clean white sheets have set a new pace for the exclusive individuals owning television sets. It should be also noted that these exclusive individuals harboring TV's are finding it almost impossible to view their own sets due to the sudden throngs of friends now invading their own rooms. We must admit that at times the technicalities of settings are most realistic in the changeover from movie to Roland's chambers.

Vociferous Reaction In Dorms

The rabble-rousing following these horror pictures is of towering magnitude. The different verbal utterences seem to amuse the students and disturb the higher echelons of the dormitories. I presume each and every Monday and Tuesday night will be the scene of this wholesale exuberance.

Shock Theatre has set a new trend and standard in the dorms. I'm so happy that there is something to look forward to as campus residents. In Sheehan Hall there are two of the most wonderful people who have invested in a machine which they call a Philco console. The tall black haired fellow seems to believe he has been the recipient of a bargain. I certainly don't mean to discourage this individual but it is to my understanding the whole thing was purchased simply in order to view "Roelun" and the exorbitant price of one hundred and sixty dollars is going a bit too far. However, if obtained — God speed to them and the second floor.

Is The End In Sight

Shock theatre brings so many viewers before the magic eye that certain rooms are voided of all furniture and martial law is enforced due to the mob rule which has to be suppressed. How long can the producers and directors of this new TV innovation, keep the different horror movies going? There must be a bottom to their shock movie barrel. If they should run out maybe coach Reagan could furnish some of his horror films.

I am most impressed with the manifestation of interest in Roland and do hope it continues. And may he become the idol of all the little tots between four and eight years of age. "Goodnight whatever you are"

Pet Peeve ...... road games

Top Weirdie Roland Played Bit Parts Here

By HARRY S. GLOVER
Staff Writer

Back in 1954 audiences at Berks County's Green Hills Theater saw a fellow by the name of John Zacherle playing parts in two of that summer's attractions, "My Three Angels" and "Dear Brutus."

Little did they reck at the time that unknown John Zacherle, bit-part actor, was in a few short years to become the sensational weirdie, Roland, of WCAU-TV's "Shock Theater" (Monday and Tuesday, 11:25 p.m.)

"Yes, I remember Berks County well," the Philadelphia-born Zacherle was telling me recently. "I spent six weeks at your Green Hills Theater.

"When I wasn't acting I was working backstage — nailing sets together, gathering props for a show, the various odd jobs of the stagehand in an enterprise of that type."

Roland

Roland (the accent goes on the back end) is making quite a dent on the viewers in this area. You hear talk of the character most everywhere you go. People seem to take to his creep getup, his unseen pal Igor and the way he breaks into the picture being shown, such as the time he peeped from behind a clump of bushes during a romantic scene. Roland fans say Roland is better than the picture, which is no great accomplishment in most cases.

Last Tuesday, for instance, it was Roland's task to gag up something entitled "Devil Girl From Mars."

"The thing has been running since last October 13," Zacherle said. "At first they were going to call me Ronald. But that didn't sound sinister enough. Then Ed Brown—he writes and produces 'Shock Theater' — came up with Roland. With the accent on the final syllable it sounded much more hideous. So I'm Roland the mad monster.

"Brown got the go-ahead for this idea from Charley Vanda, our vice president in charge of television, and they bought up a bunch of horror pictures. Frankly, most of them can use a gimmick."

Zacherle said the outfit that peddled the pictures to the station is quite happy with the Roland treatment. The series gets the viewers and that's what counts.

20,000 Letters

He said WCAU-TV got more than 20,000 letters when it invited viewers to send in three hairs apiece to stuff a pillow for the girl in the coffin, one of Roland's buddies.

Zacherle was asked if he is married.

"No. For a long time I didn't have enough to get married on. that I'm making a bucks it's almost too late. That's life, I guess."

He's 39, is a graduate of the University of Pennsylvania (1940) and a veteran free-lancer in radio and TV.

Roland, by the way, is tossing a "Ghoul's Gamble" at 1 p.m. tomorrow in WCAU-TV studios, City Line and Monument avenue, Philadelphia. All Roland addicts are invited.

6 TB **The Sunday Bulletin** Sunday, Nov. 17, 1957

Roland, the Ghoul, A Sentimental Fellow

By CAROL GELBER

ROLAND, the frock-coated, ghoulish - looking host of WCAU-TV's late night program Shock Theater, lives in a secret crypt deep in the earth.

The only entrance to it is a long, winding staircase; the only furnishings an open coffin with a "woman's" body in it (allegedly alive), skulls, tombstones, nooses, knives and other macabre appurtenances.

These are the props that greet you every Monday and Tuesday night at 11.25 on Channel 10. That's when Roland introduces the horror film of the night, tells anecdotes—and gives sly hints about the behind the - scenes activities of his "friends."

For despite his bloodcurdling surroundings, and his own eerie, unacceptable - to - humans appearance, Roland is really quite a sentimental fellow.

"I have my friends," he told a visitor to his dark quarters the other night, "and they are very dear to me. That's why I don't mind sharing them with 'humans.' "

Among his closest friends are Count Dracula, Frankenstein, the Creeper, the Invisible Man, the Mad Ghoul, Kharis the Mummy and other denizens of his half-human, half-monster world.

• • •

SENTIMENTALIST that he is, Roland keeps a journal of "memories." At the drop of a knife he will show you pictures and tell you about all the fun he's had with vampires, werewolves, murderers, monsters and ghosts.

"Then, when you see the film they are in," Roland explained genially, stroking a skull, "you can perhaps understand them and their problems better."

Roland never admits to being a vampire or other type of monster himself. He does, however, assume the deadly attributes of whoever is the star of the movie that night.

Roland is busy all the time. He is only human at night and must hide during the day. Therefore, he must get as much done in the evenings as possible.

The horror host is ageless, and keeping a scrapbook for all times is a lot of work. Keeping out the sunlight, keeping his tomb properly sepulchral is another problem. Each night, he must change the picture on the wall of whoever—or whatever —is starring in the film.

And that "woman" who keeps trying to get out of the coffin must be calmed down, by force if at all possible.

He does get some help. Igor is Roland's man servant, a loyal retainer. He has never appeared on the screen, but often you can hear him rattling his chains.

• • •

DESPITE Roland's attitude of snobbery toward persons unfortunate enough to be humans, he has built up quite a following among college students in the area.

His fan mail keeps growing. Fan clubs are being formed. "Roland" jokes, similar to the old Kilroy ones, are gaining popularity at Temple, Swarth-

HOST OF WCAU-TV's Shock Theater is Roland, half-human, half-monster, who introduces the horror films shown each Monday and Tuesday night. Roland lives in a secret crypt, furnished with coffin and gravestones.

more, Muhlenberg, Villanova, Penn and other local colleges. The station is now accepting ghoulish limericks from listeners. Roland, who finds them in skulls or caskets or any other place that's grotesque, reads the limericks on the air in his own special way.

The tall, thin host, who wears

Zacherle, a bachelor, says hi: character of Roland, grisl: though it may be, has been re ceiving proposals of marriage from college girls in the area.

Roland doesn't have too mucl time for the "daytime" people however; he doesn't like hi "human" visitors to stay to long. It was time to leave th

AS HE REALLY LOOKS. Under the plastered-down hair, bushy eyebrows and chalk-like face is a good-looking John Zacherle, who plays the part of the ghoulish Roland.

Trade Mark Registered   Wednesday, January 15, 1958

Rah-Rahs As 'Shock' Troops

Philadelphia, Jan. 14.

Colleges and universities in the Philadelphia area have upgraded WCAU-TV's "Shock Theatre" with fan clubs, fraternity house parties and recognition in the college papers. The Daily Pennsylvanian gave full story coverage with a five-pix spread. Tenor of article was "Deep in the earth, somewhere in the vicinity of WCAU, lives the coolest ghoul of them all, Roland."

WCAU-TV claims Roland to be the country's first "live" host to introduce the Screen Gems "Shock" package. Roland, in private life John Zacherle, Philly actor, with his imaginary sidekick, Igor, hosts the series from his "home," which closely resembles a crypt, complete with chains, hangman's noose and casket.

Station recently conducted a survey in five area colleges. Early reports show a student interest of more than 70% (males predominating) from some 1,400 studes interviewed.

Horror pix have sock mail pull. In answer to host's offer of free photo in exchange for three hairs from sender's head, WCAU-TV drew 1,200 pieces day after announcement. One allegedly bald-headed correspondent sent his promissory note.

Franklin & Marshall College, Lancaster, staged a horror party at which Roland was "ghost of honor." From the U. of Pennsylvania an English instructor brought her entire class to the WCAU-TV studios to study the production methods used in "Shock Theatre." Editorial (college paper) comments have been received from Millersville State Teacher's College, Villanova, Swarthmore, and Glassboro State Teachers College, N.J.

TV Star Thrills Teenagers

Roland of television's Shock Theater was greeted by more than 500 screaming youths last night in Wenzel's Auditorium, Tamaqua.

The Philadelphia television personality, who in real life is John Zacherle, a native of Flowertown, Montgomery County, signed hundreds of autographs while serving as emcee of a record dance sponsored by the Panther Valley Spartans Girls Basketball Team.

After his introduction by Bruce Frassinelli, Summit Hill, coach of the sponsoring team, Roland apologized to the youth that he was unable to bring to the dance "My Dear" and "Igor," his wife and friend, respectively.

His wife and friend, whom TV audiences never see, are comfortably quartered in a casket and dungeon in the cellar of his castle in Philadelphia, he explained. "The lights are too bright here in Tamaqua for them you know," he said.

Roland was escorted to the auditorium by two members of the state police detail at Tamaqua.

After being treated to a spaghetti dinner earlier yesterday in the home of Frassinelli, Roland was also escorted through a group of autograph seekers by police in Summit Hill.

Before appearing in Tamaqua, he was quartered in a dimly lighted garage adjoining the auditorium. "Just the kind of delightful atmosphere I enjoy," he said while waiting for his cue to appear on stage.

The 6 foot one favorite of late television viewers said he thoroughly enjoyed the hospitality of the coal fields.

MOCK HORROR: Students at Penn fraternity feign shock and terror while watching Roland's late night show at a get-together typical of Roland clubs.

From Our Readers

Correspondence for this department should be addressed to Regional Editor, TV GUIDE, 400 N. Broad St., Philadelphia 1, Pa.

Zacherle   **Young**

Please publish a picture of Ch. 10's likeable ghoul ROLAND as he looks in real life. I understand he was once a model, and am curious to see what's under all that make-up.—*Nancy Bentley, Philadelphia.* [*Pictured above is John Zacherle, alias Roland, off camera.*]

I've been reading all the bickering from your readers both pro and con about John "Roland" Zacherle. As one of his many fans, I know I'm not alone in hoping that you'll print some information about his background.—*Kathleen Smith, Collegeville, Pa.* [*Zacherle is a 39-year-old bachelor who was graduated from the U. of Pennsylvania in 1940 as an English major. He started acting with the Stagecrafters in Philadelphia and was a free-lance model and actor before assuming the ghoulish role of "Roland" on Ch. 10's Shock Theater. He is 6 feet, 1 inch tall; has blue eyes and brown hair.*]

Roland, Schmoland . . . it drives me to tears . . . to see this ghoul . . . elicit such cheers . . . His wit is gruesome . . . his talent nil . . . of Igor and mailmen . . . I've had my fill!—*Franklin Moore, Philadelphia.*

90,000 See Hero Scholarship Fund Thrill Show at Stadium

Front-row spectators clamor for autographs from television horror-actor Roland as he tours Municipal Stadium in a police motorcycle sidecar.

Roland, WCAU's "cool ghoul," pays his respects to the show's queen, Evelyn Schufrieder.

90,000 Rock and Roar To Hero Fund Thrill Show

Spectacular feats of daring blended with song and music to provide thrills and entertainment galore for more than 90,000 persons at Municipal Stadium last night.

The occasion was the fourth annual Hero Scholarship Fund Thrill Show, staged to provide scholarships for the sons and daughters of the city's uniformed men who were killed or permanently disabled while on duty.

The thrills were provided by the daredevil acts of police, firemen and park guards. Stars from the radio, television and the stage, as well as Mummer string bands handled the music and song department.

Cheers Resound

The result was a gigantic show that had something of everything for everybody. The crowd showed its enthusiasm and appreciation with resounding cheers that echoed and re-echoed through the huge outdoor theater.

The show began with a parade led by the Police and Firemen's Band escorted by mounted Fairmount Park guards. In the line of march also were the Hegeman, Quaker City, Kensington and South Philadelphia String Bands.

Then came a solemn occasion when a memorial service was held on a stage in the center of the field for the late Emanuel (Manie) Sacks, vice president of the National Broadcasting Co. and RCA-Victor.

Song of Tribute

Singer Tony Martin sang a song of tribute, and joined Theodore A. Smith, vice president of RCA, in accepting the scholarship fund's posthumous award for Sacks.

Probably the most spectacular feature of the show—trick riding by the Highway Patrol's motorcyclists—followed.

The riders executed intricate, death-defying maneuvers on their cycles at high speed. Using split-second timing, they executed figure eights, rode in formation and formed pyramids while perched on their two-wheelers.

In another act, one policeman mounted on a motorcycle rode up a ramp and then literally flew off the ramp and over 18 of his comrades lying in formation on the ground.

He cleared them, but still going at high speed had to leap off his speeding vehicle to avoid crashing into the stands.

Steve and Eydie

An interlude then followed in which singer Steve Lawrence and his wife, Eydie Gorme, NBC television stars, took over the microphone to entertain the crowd with songs.

They were introduced by Dick Clark, star of the WFIL-TV show, Bandstand, who acted as master of ceremonies.

Then came the time for an exhibition of fire-fighting and rescue work by the Fire Department.

Two aerial ladders were raised on each side of the field to a height of 85 feet in the shape of church steeples. Firemen demonstrated rope sliding techniques and how they save persons trapped by fires on upper floors.

65-Foot Leap

Another thrill was provided by Stan (Zip) Bond, a stunt man who climbed up a 65-foot tower, set himself on fire, then plunged into a flaming tank of water only six feet deep and 12 feet in diameter.

Two Swedish aerialists, Lola and Ernst Rhodin, added a touch of the circus by performing stunts on a tower 95 feet high, without benefit of safety nets.

Stars of the radio and TV who took part in the show included Roland, the "cool ghoul" of WCAU-TV; Sally Starr, Happy the Clown, Sawdust Sam and Bill Webber, of WFIL-TV; Carny C. Carny, of WCAU-TV, and the rock 'n' roll quartet, Danny and the Juniors, ABC-Paramount recording stars.

The show closed with mass singing of "God Bless America" and a spectacular fireworks display staged by Reginald E. Beauchamp, special events director of The Bulletin.

Among those participating in the ceremonies preceding the show were Mayor Dilworth, John B. Kelly, fund chairman, and James H. J. Tate, president of City Council. The invocation was given by the Rev. Marshall L. Shepard, pastor of Mt. Olivet Tabernacle Baptist Church.

Roland Fans Give Cool Ghoul Royal Ride in Kensington

The lazy routine of a summer evening in lower Kensington was shattered last night by the sudden appearance of a group of joyful mourners lugging a ghostly-white coffin through the streets.

Closer inspection by curious residents revealed that the open coffin had an occupant.

Still closer inspection showed that the mourners were boys 14 and 15 years old; that the occupant bore a resemblance to TV's cool ghoul, Roland; and that the funeral procession was marking the founding of another fan club.

Starting Fan Club

The group that carried their idol in his favorite vehicle around the intersection of Susquehanna av. and Thompson sts. so far was only the embryo of a fan club, looking for recruits.

There are now some dozen members, but no president or vice president or board of directors, and the teenage fans have not yet told their idol of their allegiance.

However, the club has big plans for the future, according to two of its members, Bob Fudala, 14, of 823 E. Thompson st., and Bill Horneff, also 14, of 732 E. Thompson st.

Plan Ghoulish Costumes

As the club grows, the boys said, they expect each member will have a ghoulish black costume equally as repulsive as Roland's.

They said they are especially anxious to outdo their patron by using face masks that glow in the dark.

Thus properly outfitted, the club will celebrate appropriate occasions, such as the full of the moon, and especially Halloween.

The coffin, which is regulation size, was built of scrap lumber by Richard Kruse, 14, of 2529 E. Norris st., with the help of other club members. It was painted white, they explained, to give a spine-chilling effect in the dark.

Stuffed with Paper

Roland, himself, the boys made by stuffing old clothes with paper. His huge and ghastly hands are actually a pair of cast-off work gloves.

The boys said they will have no trouble getting someone to play Igor, Roland's monster-sidekick, whom, of course, no one has ever seen. They are worried however, about getting someone to gurgle eerily like Roland's wife, My Dear, whose presence is sensed but seldom seen on the programs on WCAU-TV.

The club's prospective rules exclude girls.

Nevertheless, the boys think they will probably admit just one girl for the part, and they have their choice of the field: they have been besieged by applications from would-be vampires.

Roland Was Stage Mortician Before Fate Put Finger on Him

By ADRIENNE HARRISON

Until several months ago, we used to watch the "late show" on TV to see the movie. But since the arrival of "Roland" last October, all that has been changed. Now we tune in the late show to enjoy the interruptions!

It's difficult to set down the exact circumstances responsible for the almost-overnight rise to stardom of the "Cool Ghoul." Yet today, "Roland" is just about the most popular personality on television.

"How does it feel to be the present sensation of the TV industry?" we asked the personable 'casket-keeper' of WCAU's "Shock Theatre," prior to his 11:25 show one Saturday evening.

"It's pretty exciting," he admitted. "But truthfully, I can't really understand it — the way everyone is so wrapped up in the characterization, I mean. I never cashed after other stars when I was a kid, and I'm just amazed by all this attention," continued the eerie-voiced host of the perennially favorite horror movies.

According to localite Roland (he was born in Germantown), the idea for the characters — and the program — was the brainstorm of writer Ed White (who also was the voice of "Igor" and now plays "Mama Drac"). "The purpose was to give some life to the bad movies!" disclosed the dark-haired Roland.

"And we thought it would be interesting to have Igor and the Ghoul together, as a 'live' break between the movie and the commercial interruption . . . More atmosphere, you know!" explained the only 'spook' with whom this writer has had the pleasure of conversing — alive, in person, or otherwise!

Our host quickly satisfied our curiosity about where those old Frankenstein and Dracula movies originate: "Why they're from somebody's old cellar, of course!" he stated emphatically. As for Igor, "that's a Transylvanian name which comes from those old movies," Roland laughed. It's just one vicious cycle, that's all!

We were surprised to discover how Roland came to be caught right in the middle of this trend of events, as the host of "Shock Theatre." "I was walking down the hall one day," he related. "Someone from the show came up to me and said 'You're the man.' I didn't even audition for the job, but they must have figured I'd be all right for it," continued the 6-foot, 160-pound resident of Flourtown.

Their assumption was quite correct, at that. For Roland is right at home in front of TV cameras, having made his WCAU debut as the undertaker on 'Action in the Afternoon' some four years ago. He's also delivered mnay commercials on radio and TV and has, considerable acting experience via these media to his credit.

And Bucks County theatregoers — as well as "Stagecrafter" audiences — will remember his appearances before the foot-lights. Back-stage work also was included in the theatrical schedule of the tall, slim entertainer, whose interests have always centered around the stage.

'Then there was a movie I made called 'Key to Murder,'" Roland commented. "I hope they don't ever show it — it's pretty bad!" he laughed.

As the entertaining monster of TV, Roland wears his dark brown hair parted in the middle; he sports bushy gray eyebrows above his blue eyes; he uses white shoe polish on his lips and cheeks to obtain the desired effect on television. 'It tastes better than other things I could eat, like toasted spiders! he explains explicitly.

Roland's TV outfit, which he dons several hours before his program, adds immeasurably in giving him a rather sinister looking appearance, even during his infrequent exposures to bright light (as was the case when we spoke to him). It consists of a knee-length, close-fitting black coat, with a gold emblem on the front below his left shoulder; black slim trousers; black shoes, on top of which are strapped grey leather flaps. At his neck he wears a high white collar; below this, a yellow cravat with a blue pin in the center.

That's quite a get-up . . . and by the time its owner is standing behind that charming looking (!) gray casket with a few skulls on it (and with flaxen-haired "My Dear" in it!) . . . and suddenly a few eerie sounds begin emanating from hither and yon . . . with the hour being somewhere around midnight or later . . . and there's just you watching all this — well, maybe there's one other person in the room to keep you company . It's a delightfully stimulating and spooky atmosphere, wouldn't you agree?

Why it's just what the doctor (the witch-doctor, that is!) prescribed for all of us wide-awake advocates of TV at those bewitching hours surrounding midnight!

But what is there for a Ghoul to do during those non-ghoul hours? "Why I eat and sleep like everybody else, of course!" Roland assures us.

In fact, he says that when he is on the street (Imagine Roland being that disloyal to the "Ghostly Association of Ghouls" and admitting to being sociable and human! Indeed!) he isn't recognized too often. Of course he wouldn't be, if he insists on letting himself appear human and earthly-loking, like the rest of us!

For example, he admits to wearing his hair as an ordinary male would. "I part it on the side, like you do, my dear," he said to this writer. And Roland also claims to have merely normal sized eye-brows, as well as an unchalked face, when he's not hosting his show. Why, the man is shocking even when he's not on "Shock Theatre!"

But somehow it just doesn't seem possible to many individuals that Roland is a person . . . a real honest-to-goodness human being. One young boy asked Roland if he ever goes out in the sunlight. 'Well, you donT THINK I live in that casket ALL the time, do you?" Roland replied, as he peered menacingly down at the youngster, who was completely confused by this time!

Possessor of a magnificent satirical wit, as well as a genuine enjoyment of people, Roland has this to say about his thousands of followers: "We enjoy their enjoying us."

And there certainly is sufficient tangible evidence that his fans do enjoy him. Not only does the host of "Shock Theatre" receive an estimated 2000 fan letters per week, but there are also approximately 800 Roland fan clubs throughout Philadelphia and surrounding areas — with members from just about everywhere! And then there are the two girls who offered to market the products sponsoring the show!

That's quite a following, made even more fantastic when you realize that his show celebrated its seven-month birthday only last week.

The man who made ghosts, ghouls, caskets, amoebas, as well as invisible people and dogs — an integral part of our lives is 39-year-old John Zacherle. Well-accustomed to delivering a convincing performance on stage, John is now proving most definitely, to the delight of his audience, that by allowing your imagination to work overtime, the unreal can become very real, indeed.

John had a seemingly difficult time selecting one event he could consider outstanding' in his career. At last, after several minutes of deep, concentrated thought, his blue eyes lit up in their inimitable ghoulish way. "I remember we had 'Open House' here at the studio," Roland recalled. "We anticipated about two or three thousand people, and close to 13,000 showed up. That certainly was unexpected, as well as exciting, I must say."

The crowd appeared to include people of all ages — young teenagers, high school and college students, even parents and grandparents. It looks as though everyone's interested in meeting a real live ghoul these days!

College students seem to dig the "Cool Ghoul" the most; especially those at the University of Pennsylvania: It's not at all surprising, however, when you consider the fact that right now "Roland" is that institution's most popular alumnus!

"Yes, I majored in English there after graduating from Germantown High School," related the celebrated hearse-host. "Little did I know then that I'd be working with amoebas and caskets!" the ex-Germantownite exclaimed.

Is John married? "Not on your sweet life!" he informed us, with that ghoulish gleam re-appearing in his eye once more.

John related that the "Roland" characterization does not disappear as soon as his show is over; but rather, it remains with him all the time. "Roland is always on my mind," he declared.

And many other minds as well, he might have added, for he has received offers to appear as a guest on many other shows. "However, most of these invitations are for Friday and Saturday evening," he said. "Even though these shows are over quite a while before my show begins, there are rehearsals and many other things that I must do during these hours. So unfortunately I can't accept most of the invitations," Roland explained.

Roland mentioned that the program director decides on the films to be shown on "Shock Theatre." But the program's host added that he often makes suggestions to vary the movies which we see. "It can get monotonous watching the same type of film week after week. So we try to change them as often as we can," Roland continued.

He also does some of his own script-writing. "But what eventually comes out is half Ed White and half me!" he added.

"Who decided on using the name 'Roland' in the first place I inquired.

"Oh, that was actually an accident," my host disclosed. The name was originally supposed to be 'Ronald'. But the announcer came out with 'Roland', with the accent on the first syllable, the way the name is usually pronounced. Somehow that was too plain, so we tried emphasizing the second syllable. Everyone liked it, so it remained 'Roland'," the cool ghoul went on.

Roland was the country's first "live" host to introduce this present series of Frankenstein movies on television. Each Friday and Saturday evening, Roland welcomes all of us to his "friendly, cozy WCAU-TV domicile." Here, providing the proper atmosphere to allow maximum enjoyment of those fascinatingly horrible films, are chains, hangmen's noose, the now famous casket, skulls, and other associated and equally pleasurable accoutrements. Could one possibly dream of any more exciting furnishings in one's home???!!

In the available hours between commitments at his TV "Living Quarters" and his real life suburban residence, John engages in many interesting diversions. These include modeling for magazine advertisements; gardening (which he considers his main hobby); and activities related to his chosen entertainment profession.

So it seems as if Roland, the Coolest of all Ghouls, really does possess a very human side after all. Despite his close association with such dubious characters as those with whom he is seen twice each week in his TV abode, he's just like many of us.

Except that before the arrival of Roland, who among us would have dared take leave of our friends by expressing Roland' priceless exit line — "Goodnigh WHATEVER you are!"

Screening TV

Just Can't Dig Roland

By HARRY HARRIS

NOW that he's become such a celebrated spook, with national nods in magazines like the Saturday Evening Post and TV Guide, we thought we'd better take another look at WCAU-TV's cool ghoul, Roland.

If this be teen-age treason, make the most of it! On the basis of quick looks at "Shock Theater" Friday and Saturday, we couldn't care—or scare—less.

Maybe every little mumble has a meaning all its own, but—despite the graveyard atmosphere—we didn't dig. A soap opera-like summary of earlier innings would certainly help late arrivals to Roland's revels.

Anyway, on Friday, we gathered that Igor, down in the bowels of the building, was making something to power space ships, and that Roland was having a tug-of-war with My Dear for a huge bomb nestled in her coffin. On Saturday (congratulations!) Roland seemed to have cleaned up his spouse's messy haunts.

John Zacherle, the human hidden under the Roland trappings, looked up at one point Friday to chortle, "I'm getting through to you, h'ain't I?" Frankly, John—no!

* * *

MAYBE we just aren't attuned to these ghost-to-ghost programs. During WACU-TV's "Block Party" Saturday afternoon, host Hy Lit was gifted with a package containing "all you need to be a charter member of the Roland Fan Club."

The ingredients i n c l u d e d Igor's whip, a map of Transylvania, a voodoo doo doll, mummy wrappings, type-A blood (type Oh! would seem more appropriate), Roland's pet, a spider's egg, bat wing confetti, a photo of the Great Monster himself and the loony like.

Obviously Roland's more dedicated "people" live in a realm out of THIS world!

Our reason for looking in on "Block Party" Saturday was to witness the world premiere of the Block Rock, a dance specially created for the 90-minute show. As demonstrated by the Latinaires, it seemed danceable enough, but when Lit solicited the reaction of his teen-age audience, there were only a few weak huzzahs.

The program itself is Dick Clark's "American Bandstand" out-of-doors, with a few slightly different trimmings and frequent use of an overhead camera.

One thing that impressed us was the vigor with which the teen-agers rocked and rolled. Noel Coward has it that mad dogs and Englishmen go out in the midday sun. But not even THEY would try dancing in it!

* * *

A Cool Ghoul Holds School

Top row, from left to right: Barbara Leopold, Gail Johnson, Mary Lee Newbold, Ellen Leopold, Robin Harmer, Candy Keel, Tony Lame, Michael Suehle. Middle row, from left to right: Elizabeth Hamilton, Henry Dorsey, Kevin McKinney, Tod Lueders, Logie Bullitt. Front row, left to right: Peter Suehle, Francie Wells, ROLAND, Bonnie Bullitt, Cathy Keel.

End of the Line

The witches and demons of Chestnut Hill could be heard frolicking about in an especially gay mood last week when Roland came to town in his official capacity as cool ghoul. Ugly Roland is attractive John Zacherle of Flourtown whose personality is really on the quiet side and whose manner is actually mild. We ought to know! We spent most of an afternoon with him and after a fun interview we found out what our favorite horror with humor is really like.

The facts are these. He is thirty-nine. He went to Germantown High School and received his B.A. degree at the University of Pennsylvania. During World War II he was a captain in the army. A civilian again, he began his acting career at Chestnut Hill's own Stagecrafters. From there he went into television westerns at WCAU. Last October, however, he was appointed hair raising host of Shock Theatre, which is a later movie show specializing in spooky stories. He drives a black Ford, his favorite sport is golf and a favorite hobby is gardening. (Can you imagine Roland tending flowers?)

Naturally, we questioned him mostly about his "television self. Before his show goes on, he parts his hair in the middle, pats powder on his sideburns and applies white shoe polish to his lips. Thusly, he is transformed into ROLAND!!!!! Now, in front of the camera he usually conducts experiments often as not on human brains.

(Well the brains are cauliflowers when in season or cabbages). The human nerve that he extracts from the brain is really a nine foot string, and his pet amoeba who has run away, is really a blob of jello wrapped in gauze, He has a wife named "My Dear" whom he keeps locked in a box (she manages to spit out at him though) and a forever unseen pet named Igor.

At first he wrote his own shows but now is so busy that the station has had to hire a writer and lately a special secretary to handle all his mail. He asked for each viewer to send him three human hairs for a pillow he was making. He got 23,000 answers and many fans sent him whole pony tails! He made the "Dinner with Drac" record which is a big hit. Pictures of him and provided by him are available to those writing and requesting them.

John Zacherle's plans for the future include more records and fortunately for fun loving Philadelphians more of Shock Theatre on Friday and Saturday nights. He will also be busy doing benefit shows and this week did one at the request of an ardent fan — a minister.

Mary H. Bullitt

CITIZEN OF THE WEEK

John Zacherle, a Flourtown resident, a good looking, rather mild-mannered young man who gives the impression of being a pleasantly successful bond salesman, is the "Cool Ghoul," Roland, who has captured the imagination, if not the heart, of local late-night television viewers.

Zacherle, who undergoes a curious Jeckyll-Hyde like transformation each Friday and Saturday night for WCAU's "Shock Theater," has brought new life to some old and rather tired movies with his experiments on the human brain (cauliflower), heart (beef kidney), and an outsized amoeba (a large platter of gelatine).

He is also assisted in his visits to such old friends as Frankenstein, the Wolf Man, the Mummy, Dracula, and other charming characters by My Dear, his vampire wife from Transylvania, and Igor, a strange creature who dotes on postman, both of whom are unseen.

Zacherle, as Roland, the master of ceremonies of these other-wordly activities, has captured the loyalty of his fans to such an extent that when the station held an open house in February, over 12,000 persons attended. When he asked for three human hairs from each viewer, he received hairs from 23,000 fans and an I. O. U. from a bald, but dedicated, follower.

Zacherle, under his own name, has made a record on the Cameo label called "Dinner With Drac." On this record he reads ghoulish poems and limericks over a wild and raucous rock and roll background. The record sales have reached close to a quarter of a million, and another record is expected shortly.

His previous experience does not exactly seem the type to prepare him for his present role as ambassador without portfolio for the weird and strange creatures of the night. A former resident of Germantown, Zacherle attended Germantown High School and the University of Pennsylvania, where he received an A. B. degree in English literature.

A former member of the University's ROTC group, he quickly entered the Army when World War II began. As a captain in the Quartermaster Corps, he saw service in England, Italy and North Africa. Following the war,

JOHN ZACHERLE

he became a major in the Army Reserve.

In the years after the war Zacherle tried to obtain as much theatrical experience as possible. He did much radio work, both as an announcer and actor; was a member of the Stagecrafters, a Chestnut Hill group; and even did some summer stock.

In 1954, he appeared in WCAU's "Action In The Afternoon," a weekly serial western which attracted a great deal of attention. Since then he has appeared in the Benjamin Franklin series on Television, many commercials for both radio and TV, and industrial films. Curiously enough, during this time, Zacherle, who portrays this frightening character with a light-hearted touch, won first prize for his setting at the Philadelphia Flower Show.

When the Roland character was suggested to the station, Zacherle was thought of as ideal man and selected without even an audition. Since October 7, 1957, his fiendish glee in entertaining his audience, "whatever you are," has made him the most talked of personality in the Philadelphia area.

THE AMBLER GAZETTE (PENNSYLVANIA)
APRIL 17, 1958

Seats to Spare

Horror Movie Fans All but Stampede To See Their TV Ghoul Hero, Roland

A screeching crowd of teenagers jammed 9th street in Allentown last night to see Roland — one of America's most popular television ghouls.

One paddy wagon, a cruiser car, motorcycle, five patrolmen, two firemen and a fire inspector were sent into action to keep things orderly in front of the Earle Theater.

The crowd is believed to have reached about 600 at one point. Everyone wanted a seat. As it turned out, there were more than a hundred seats left over.

Highpoint in the action came shortly after the lobby door was opened. For a few minutes ticket takers were nearly trampled by the shouting youths. The onslaught for seats was quickly quieted down.

Bounced

One person was hustled out of the theater after he tried to slip under a rope and push his way into the inner lobby. Police described him as married with one child. He was released.

Once seated, the crowd was noisy but not violent.

The show was by far the most lively of three held during the day. Roland's appearances were presented by Gene Kaye of Allentown radio station WHOL.

Roland was escorted into Allentown by two police motorcycles. His three-car caravan—with escort—parked in front of a Hamilton street restaurant where a crowd of about 500 persons gathered to watch Roland interviewed on a WHOL morning program.

The TV character also drew quite a few spectators during a promotion appearance at a local floor covering store. He is said to have signed about 360 autographs during that appearance.

A not-too-old science fiction movie called "Kronos" preceded Roland's appearance during the three shows.

Big Change

In a backstage dressing room a Jekyll and Hyde scene was taking place.

John Zacherle, a goodlooking, dark-haired and mild-mannered man in his twenties opened his black leather makeup case. Within a half-hour he was Roland — gruesome - looking, gray- - haired and fiendish.

Half way through the changeover, with grease pencil in hand, Zacherle emitted several wolf wails into his backstage microphone. His young audience roared.

Zacherle told The Morning Call he is interested in putting Roland into media other than television. He mentioned films as a possibility. Recently, he made a recording called "Dinner with Drac" which sold about 250,000 copies.

Before Roland was introduced to nighttime TV audiences last October, Zacherle played minor television roles. "Once I played an undertaker on an afternoon program," he said. "Maybe that's how all this started."

The Roland character was the brainstorm of staff members at WCAU-TV in Philadelphia. As Zacherle explains it: "Basically, it was that the horror movies we used were really terrible. Roland brightens them up."

Within the nine months that Shock Theater has been on television, Roland's popularity has increased tremendously. He has fan clubs operating throughout Eastern Pennsylvania and elsewhere and has achieved top ratings for his twice-weekly programs.

The ghoul from Transylvania has quite an effect on audiences. During the second show yesterday a 7-year-old Allentown boy reportedly went screaming full-speed out of the theater when Roland made his entrance.

A person who stopped him outside quoted the boy as sobbing: "He can't get me while I'm watching television. But here he can."

FRIDAY, AUGUST 29, 1958

Cool Ghoul Roland Draws 1,000 to Exchange Club Record Hop

Roland, the cool ghoul who has captured the imagination of the teenagers with his antics as master of ceremonies on television's Shock Theatre, entertained more than 1,000 young guests at the Convention Hall here Monday night.

The cellar-dwelling spinner of fantastic yarns visited the resort to help the Exchange Club of Ocean City to swell its scholarship fund, which offers $900 a year financial assistance to Ocean City High School graduates in college.

Roland entertained his fans, ranging from pre-teen youngsters to college youths, with accounts of his problems with his shrewish wife, My Dear, and his monstrous friend, Igor, whom he keeps caged in a sub-cellar.

With a coffin as a podium, Roland signed his autograph on hundreds of his photos, admission tickets, scraps of papers and on shirts and blouses of his fans.

Prior to the show, the Philadelphia showman was guest at the dinner-meeting of the Exchange Club at Plymouth Inn. His legal name is John Zacherie, and despite his ghoulish appearance on the television screen he is a handsome Princeton-type young man.

His power of attraction for the younger set was testified to by the fact that continued rainfall Monday evening failed to keep a capacity crowd of youngsters from coming out and meeting him personally.

4 H **The Evening Bulletin** Thurs., June 19, 1958

In Our Town

By Earl and Anne Selby

The Star . . .

THE ANNUAL PICNIC for the old folks at the city's home—Riverview—had a hayride, games of chance (where nobody could lose), a tent supper complete with pizza.

But can you guess what scored the biggest hit?

It was the appearance of television's liveliest ghoul, Roland, who delighted the oldsters with tales of Transylvania, spooky relatives and old friends.

IGOR'S CHUM

RADIO AND TELEVISION

"The Cool Ghoul" On Clark's Show

By JAMES A. GOURGOURAS

TODAY'S TOPPERS — Spearfishing is the topic of an illustrated lecture at 6:30 on "Kingdom of the Sea" via Channel 5.

Dick Clark's music package at 7:30 via Channels 5 and 9.

Perry Como's guest at 8 on Channels 4 and 10 is Kate Smith, and his opening production number: "Miami."

Jimmy Durante is the "Club Oasis" star at 9 on Channels 4 and 10.

Newlywed Gisele MacKenzie has Japanese actress Miyoshi Umeki visiting her at 9:30 on Channels 4 and 10.

Guess who visits Paladin at 10 on Channels 7 and 12 in "Have Gun, Will Travel"? None other than Victor McLaglen, old-time movie star.

Mike Wallace has Tennessee Williams on his interview show at 10 on Channels 5 and 9; Wallace plans asking Williams why his plays are obsessed with tragedy and despair, and why he — a Southern writer — has never tackled the race question.

"COOL GHOUL" — We're going to catch Dick Clark's telecast at 7:30 tonight (Channels 5 and 9) in order to see for ourselves the "Cool Ghoul" . . . He's the man who plattered the talk-about record, "Dinner with Drac," that local deejays are featuring around town . . . John Zacherle is the gent's real name, and he has a show of his own on a Philadelphia TV station . . . This will be his first dip into a national network.

JOHN ZACHERLE
Has Sister in Worcester

SISTER HERE — Zacherle has a sister living here, Mrs. Arthur K. Haddad of 14 Oxford St., and she's the one who tipped us off on the "Cool Ghoul" label, which she attributed to Clark . . . No matter what the name, it ought to be worth catching for his "Shock Theater" series on WCAU—TV in Philadelphia casts him as a Dracula-like attired gent who receives such assorted gifts from "admirers" as pickled hearts, skulls, nooses, and deathhead masks!

TV Roundup

'Cool Ghoul' To Play Guest And Plug Disc

Philadelphia

ONE local teen-age favorite will guest on another's network show Saturday night—but John Zacherle, who portrays WCAU-TV's "cool ghoul," Roland, still doesn't know if he'll appear on ABC's "Dick Clark Show" as John Zacherle or as Roland.

The decision will probably be made for him Friday when Charles Vanda, the station's TV vice president, returns to his desk. The Roland monicker and shenanigans are WCAU - TV's property.

Zacherle will appear with WFIL - TV's Clark to boost his two-week-old Cameo disk, "Dinner With Drac," a

ROLAND

mixture of rock 'n' roll music and spoken "sick" limericks.

It was cut by Zacherle under his real name and reissued in a toned-down version, at Clark's suggestion, after a Cleveland station decided it was too gory for the squeamish.

The record (available with and without "Igor" on the flip side) has been catching on with teenagers here, in Cleveland and in Chicago. Zacherle has received bids from Patti Page's "The Big Record" and other network programs, but so far is committed only to Saturday's appearance.

ZACH: *"Dick Clark was a fan and he knew there was a big craze among the high school and college kids in town when I was doing Roland. He also knew that I'd done the song 'Dinner with Drac' and it was up in the top ten, so Dick made it a point to have me do the song on his show. He was a very nice guy to hang out with."*

CHANNEL CHAT

Roland's Dick Clark Show Visit Stirs Up a Ghoulish Hassle

QUITE a hassle has developed over "cool ghoul" Roland's scheduled appearance on the Dick Clark Show tomorrow night.

The character was created by WCAU to host its Shock Theater presentations of weird late-night feature movies. Almost immediately, Roland, portrayed by actor John Zacherle, became a hit with the high school and college set.

A few weeks ago, Roland, using his right name, recorded "Dinner With Drac," an eerie disc which seems destined to hit the national best seller lists. There are two versions of it, one less grisly than the other.

On the strength of the record's success, Clark signed Zacherle for his new ABC show

(7.30, Channel 6 here), and announced last week that Roland would be a guest.

WCAU doesn't mind Zacherle appearing as Zacherle, but reportedly has protested against his using the cadaverous Roland make-up and costumes identified with his Shock Theater appearances.

Meanwhile, Clark is reported to be miffed that his own station, WFIL, won't allow Zacherle to appear on Dick's daily American Bandstand program, either as Zacherle or Roland. To okay such a guest spot, the station would in effect be plugging the personality of a rival channel.

Dick Clark thought the original "Dinner with Drac" was "too ghoulish" and had Zach record new, toned-down lyrics and lip-sync them on the show.

* * *

ROLAND, WCAU-TV's "Cool Ghoul," made his network debut Saturday night on the ABC show hosted by WFIL-TV's Dick Clark looking like Roland but answering to the name of John Zacherle.

That was the compromise worked out just one day earlier after much soul-searching, by the Channel 10 braintrusters who invented the eerie character to introduce their "Shock Theater" chillers.

Clark gave his fellow Philadelphian a big sendoff, dubbing Zacherle's "Dinner with Drac" "the biggest novelty hit of 1958." It turned out to be a wild rock 'n roll number which quieted down from time to time when Zacherle cracked a gory gag.

The cadaverous Roland was given an all-star supporting cast

Around the Dials
Roland's 'Guests' Overrun WCAU

By BOB WILLIAMS

THE fabled locusts of China couldn't have done a more thorough stripping job than the human species that invaded WCAU's gleaming modern studios on City Line av. on Saturday.

We refer to the uncounted thousand of teenagers and pre-teeners — predominantly male—who swarmed into the spacious building to pay hysterical homage to the ghoulish TV personality known as Roland. The station had invited fans to an open house, and was figuring on a big crowd, but hardly a mob scene.

When the last lad had departed, an inventory showed that nearly every item of a Roland lobby display had been swiped, a door had been unhinged, the railing in front of the radio and TV control room badly bent, the shrubbery ruined. Also one Lower Merion Township policeman was reported nursing the bruises of a once-over lightly trampling.

If the station brass is bleeding over the shambles, they must be bleeding happily. An incident such as Saturday's is indisputable evidence that what started as a gimmick has mushroomed into a wildly successful Presley-like phenomena without precedent in local TV, so far as we recall.

We'll let the psychologists figure out why these youngsters have become so enraptured of Roland's grisly make-believe which spices the Shock Theater horror films on Monday and Tuesday nights at 11.25.

But from the entertainment angle, Roland's astonishing hold over the kids is proof again that even experienced showmen can't always predict when or where the magic will strike. When the station hired Actor John Zacherle for the ghoul bit, it was conceived as a come-on for the spooky films.

The tail is now wagging the dog. Roland is the smash hit; the movies are mere framework for his weird nonsense.

Saturday's hoopla underscores something else: that a lot of youngsters are staying up awfully late these nights.

To get an idea how many fans were watching The Shock Theatre, WCAU invited them to visit Roland's set. Thousands arrived, tying up local traffic. Zach: "I was standing on my set, which was all lit up, and people would wander through and I would talk to them and they'd take pictures. It was an amazing experience." In reaction to WCAU's estimate of 12,000, Zach wrote to a fan: "I never counted that many — but it was a mob!

"They were trying very hard to get a breakfast food sponsor or something for Shock Theatre, and they didn't get one. They had this big event where all the people showed up, and they still couldn't sell the show to an advertiser."

Fans Overwhelm Roland At Hall

Not even Transylvania, famed as the home of werewolves, vampires and other sorts of off-beat citizens could have exceeded the wild welcome extended to Roland here last night at the Garden State Home Show in Convention Hall.

Things started quietly for Roland, eerie TV emcee of a horror film show. Attired in his usual macabre get-up, complete with coffin, he greeted a crowd of young admirers and obligingly signed autographs for them.

But the crowd swelled by leaps and bounds and soon a milling throng described as "thousands" of youthful fans swirled around Roland, and, carried away by the spirit of the things, began shredding Roland's attire for souvenirs.

Roland took to flight up balcony stairs and from his high vantage point watched as police reinforcements quieted his exuberant devotees.

A SPECIAL MESSAGE TO OUR AUDIENCE FROM WCAU-TV

The entire staff of WCAU-TV is sincerely sorry for the inconveniences you may have suffered when you came to WCAU Television Center Saturday to meet "ROLAND", star of our "SHOCK THEATRE".*

While we are deeply grateful to the more than 12,000 of you who came to Roland's "Open House" we regret that we were unable to accommodate all of you in comfort.

Thank you again for this overwhelming expression of interest in our programs and personalities.

WCAU-TV

Channel 10

DNESDAY MORNING, MARCH 26, 1958

TV Digest

Ghoulish MCs Gleam In Shock Show Roles, Overshadow Films

HERE'S what some of the Nation's magazines are saying this week about television:

TV GUIDE: Three seasons ago station KABC-TV in Los Angeles introduced an eerie female named Vampira as hostess for a series of horror movies . . . Like a good ghost, Vampira departed after stealing a few headlines.

Last fall, when the "Shock Theater" package of such old horror movies as "Frankenstein," "Dracula," "The Invisible Man" and various "Sons" thereof started the rounds, stations set about digging up weird personalities to give the films that nice extra touch of spine-tingling horror —a spooktacular collection of leering, smirking, black-clad other-world characters.

ROLAND

These creeps (or more politely, hosts) have now become the tail that wags the dog, attracting more of a following than the films themselves.

In staid Philadelphia, for example, a weirdie named Roland (he has an unseen creature named Igor who devours mailmen) presides at WCAU-TV.

Roland (actually actor John Zacherle) is typical of the "monsters of ceremonies" who spend their TV lives amid coffins, rattling chains, werewolves and other goodies.

On Chicago's WBKB, for instance, Terry Bennett has an assistant, a red-haired model named Dorothy Johnson, whose sole function is to scream. . . . On one occasion, he cut out a woman's heart (slab of beef liver), listened to it beat and sent it to a Lonely Hearts Club. He also serves "shocktails" made of embalming fluid.

A Miss Tarantula Ghoul operates at KPTV, Portland, Ore.

Then there's George Byram, of KBTV, Denver, Col., who roams catacombs filled with madmen and monsters. He also has made himself disappear bit by bit and, while headless, has delivered commercials.

WMBD-TV's Milton Budd introduces Peoria, Ill., to his "son" —created by superimposing his own head in his hand.

Many of the horror hosts are adored by large and growing fan —or rather, fan-atic—clubs, have been honored guests at school social functions and have ratings that are the despair of their saner competition.

* * *

Exchange Invites 'Roland' to City

Spookmaster Booked For Aug. 25 Benefit

The rock 'n roll concert by Bill Haley and His Comets here on August 16 will be trumped by the ghoulish antics of Roland on August 25, Exchange Club President Philip Turner announced this week.

The Exchange Club of Ocean City will sponsor the appearance of the recording star popular with the teenage set and the visit to the resort by the star of television's late evening spook shows.

The events will benefit the Exchange Club's Scholarship Fund, which is committed to $900 a year for the financial assistance of Ocean City High School graduates pursuing college educations.

Haley and His Comets will give two performances at the high school auditorium on August 16 at 8 p. m. and at 9:30 p. m. Tickets are available from members of the Exchange Club, and ticket booths will be set up next week in various parts of the city.

Roland will be in Convention Hall on Monday evening, August 25, with his outworldish friends, "My Dear" and "Igor." The TV spookmaster will direct a recording session for dancing and will entertain guests with his fantastic tales, the latest of which is Igor's flight into outer space.

The National flower of the United States is the goldenrod.

Ocean City Sentinel Ledg 8-9-58

ABOVE: *Zach on his WCAU set. The TV station's building was newish and had ridiculously high ceilings.* ZACH: *"Frank Lloyd Wright came in to see this building, and his remark was, 'What a waste of space!'"*

Page Thirty-Two

Youthful Fans Of Roland Stir WCAU, Police

Fans of Roland, sinister host of a late-night horror movie show on WCAU-TV, gave Lower Merion police cause for alarm over the weekend.

Irate fans of the ghoulish Roland, whose real name is John Zacherle, threatened to stone the television station's studios in Bala on both Fri and Saturday nights aft-er their hero's baleful coun-tenance failed to haunt their screens last week.

Lower Merion police were called out to guard the build-ing both nights after the stu-dio received a number of threatening phone calls. No incidents were reported, how-ever.

Roland, who has become enormously popular with both teen-agers and the local col-lege crowd with his off-beat manner and a rock 'n roll re-cording called Dinner With Drac, stalked off last week after a salary disagreement.

Roland has been replaced by My Dear, a female ghoul who now kids fans into think-ing that she has Roland stow-ed away in a crypt, using an ax occasionally to keep him under dontro.

(If this doesn't win him a raise and network status, nothing ever will.)

TV Roundup

My Dear, Igor! Roland Rests 'In His Coffin'

Philadelphia

ALTHOUGH Roland, accord-ing to a WCAU-TV spokes-man, is "in the coffin at the mo-ment" and may reappear soon as host of the station's Friday and Saturday "Shock Theater," whether the "cool ghoul" will be enacted by John Zacherle is still up in the air.

Zacherle, who has become a teen-age fad through his Chan-nel 10 appearances and his "Dinner With Drac" recording, left his midnight crypt last week after a disagreement over ad-ditional daytime duties.

Negotiations are still under way, the spokesman said.

Meanwhile, the hosting duties have been taken over by Rol-and's feminine sidekick, My Dear, who's being portrayed by actress Jean Ziegler.

A number of Roland's parti-sans conducted a pilgrimage to the WCAU studios Saturday, to protest their favorite's absence.

Laurie London, the 12-year-old

WILLIAM J. LLOYD

Roland Let Out

WCAU Asks Police For Protection

The WCAU television studios on City Line were threatened with damage on Friday and Saturday nights of last week, and the Low-er Merion police were appealed to for protection.

The threats were received by telephone from teen-age fans of Roland, a ghoulish character idol-ized by midnight television view-ers, chiefly immature youngsters.

The Roland fans are displeased because their imitation Boris Kar-loff has been let out by WCAU-TV. He thought he was worth more money, but WCAU didn't think so. Now, instead of Roland whacking an unseen female for the edification of teen-agers, a female whacks at an unseen Ro-land, it is said. The fans do not like this.

Despite the threats to hurl stones at the studio building and do other harm, the police saw no sign of a Roland fan in the vicin-ity of the building.

Rifle Shot Kills

ZACH: *"I made the Cameo Parkway record 'Dinner with Drac' and WCAU was upset because they didn't think I had the right to do it. Cameo Parkway used my own name [John Zacherle], not the name that I was using on TV [Roland] — but WCAU took me off the air! What a stupid thing to do. I had no contract, I was getting paid the minimum to do this show late at night. They should have had me sign a contract, but they didn't know that the show was going to be successful. It was top-rated a few weeks after I started. What an absurd thing, to take somebody from a hit show off the air because I made a recording using my own name! Crazy! Of course there was a big uproar from the fans, and I was back on the air the next week."*

WESTERN UNION
TELEGRAM
W. P. MARSHALL, PRESIDENT

1201

WUH361 P LLB369 PD=DUPLICATE OF TELEPHONED TGM= PHILADELPHI

IA PENN 25 1122PME= JOHN ZACHERLE=CARE WCAU CHANNEL 10 PHILA

=WELCOME BACK DARLING LOVE=OLGA=•••(1134 PME APR25 58)

WUH017 P LLA43 (P LLB385) CGN PD=PHILADELPHIA PENN 25

1140PME=JOHN ZACHERLE= CARE WCAU TV PHILA=DEAR MR ZACHERLE

WARMEST CONGRATULATIONS ON YOUR TRIUMPHFUL RETURN BEST WISHES

FOR INFINITE CONTINUED SUCCESS LETTER FOLLOWS• YOUR FRIENDS=

STEPHEN AND JEANNETTE THOMAS=(38)••

•(119 AME APR26 58) M

John Zacherle Is Back as Roland

F   31

The Evening Bulletin
Friday, April 25, 1958

JOHN ZACHERLE will be back as Roland on Channel 10's Shock Theater tonight at 11.25.

Zacherle quit, reportedly over a salary dispute, before last weekend's shows. Since then, the station has been bombarded with hundreds of protests from the "cool ghoul's" teenage fans, some of whom circulated petitions in their neighborhoods.

A spokesman for the station said today that its differences with Zacherle have been resolved.

Actually, Zacherle missed only two programs—Friday's and Saturday's — since the horror movies he hosts are aired only on those days.

Out of "spook" uniform, John Zacherle—alias Roland, host of WCAU-TV's "Shock Theater"—admires a gift from one of his admirers, a pickled heart. It joins skulls and noose among his eerie souvenirs.

Man About Town

By Frank Brookhouser

22 G **The Evening Bulletin** Mon., August 11, 1958

CHILDREN'S LIBRARIANS are accustomed to the fact that some of the weightier classics have a habit of sitting on the bookshelves.

But one of these, "The Song of Roland," the great saga of French chivalry, has been mysteriously moving back into circulation at the Free Library of Philadelphia and its branches in our town.

The only explanation members of the Free Library can provide is that some of our town's youngsters have been staying up late enough to view "Roland" and his horror movies on WCAU-TV.

Having stayed up late enough to watch "Roland," the staff members have concluded, the youngsters have innocently confused his world of ghouls and vampires with the old story of Roland, the valiant knight.

Thus far the library has received no complaints. No outright complaints, that is. There has, however, been a slight note of confusion.

TV Digest

Viewers Flip Over Vampires And Monsters

HERE'S what some of the Nation's magazines are saying this week about television:

SATURDAY EVENING POST: A new scourge has hit the land. A large, untidy package of ghouls, werewolves, vampires, Frankensteins and other assorted monsters has been flung into our living rooms via that electronic marvel, the television set.

The whole thing has become far too big for a 21-inch screen. What started as a revival of a few old horror movies on TV has now spilled over into other aspects of our national life.

America has become monster-conscious. Or, as they say in the trade, "horror's hot!"

The current madness (was kicked off) by the revival of the old movies, "King Kong" two seasons ago. That we were in for another wave of macabre nonsense was immediately apparent to the astute when the showing of the picture on television attracted one of the largest audiences of all time.

ROLAND

In most cases, a brand-new and highly potent ingredient was added to spark the boom—the local, home-grown "monster of ceremonies."

Of all the cities that have flipped for Frankenstein, none has done so more completely than the staid and proper city of Philadelphia. A mad, bumbling, but somehow charming ghoul by the name of Roland . . . has completely captivated the City of Brotherly Love.—ROUL TUN-LEY

FRATERNITY MEMBERS at Franklin and Marshall College in Lancaster carry Roland (John Zacherle), host of Channel 10's Shock Theater, to their frat house in a coffin, one of the props the 'Cool Ghoul' uses.

Are you coming to see us in Henryville?

'Roland' Dead Drunk? (A Grave Offense)

"Roland" made the hearings at 22d St. and Hunting Park Ave. police station today a piece of ghostly business.

Magistrate Nathan Beifel was horrified. The crowd of hangers on was stunned. Because of defendant John Zawislak.

HE WAS WEARING a black cutaway coat, just like Roland, TV's midnight ghoulish horror movie host.

He also had on gray spats, like Roland.

His hair, parted in the middle, was plastered to his scalp, as if he had gotten up a sweat robbing graves.

A lacy handkerchief flapped from his coat pocket. It was stained blood red.

Tough "Biff" Beifel stuttered "W-who are you?"

"I'm supposed to be Roland," said

Zawislak, 20, of 4532 Wilde St. He explained he's an entertainer. Dresses like Roland—his idol. He travels between bars, puts on an act for free drinks. He'd gotten too many, was charged with intoxication.

BEIFEL, no late movie watcher: "Who's Roland?"

Zawislak: horrified, "He's a television entertainer who puts people in coffins."

Beifel: "Why don't you wash that make-up off your face?"

Zawislak: "In this costume, without make-up, people would think I'm nuts."

Beifel: "What'll you do if I discharge you on this drunk charge?"

Zawislak: "I'll go back to my coffin for a good day's sleep."

Beifel: "Go ahead." He went.

Roland Stages Riot

Photo by John W. McClellan

Our beloved "Roland" takes part in a riot which was promoted by the Saturday Evening Post in order to snap pictures for a feature story it has planned for the early fall. The magazine trucked a load of children to the scene in Flourtown where the ghoul began to weave his eerie spell.

Advance Editorial Information

THE SATURDAY EVENING POST

August 16, 1958

Ghouls!
Werewolves!
Vampires!

TV's MIDNIGHT MADNESS

By Roul Tunley

What's behind television's astonishing boom in ghouls, monsters and other horrible creatures? Here are the practitioners—and some psychological interpretations—of "TV's Midnight Madness".

Promotion Suggestions: All national display material will feature this article as well as newspaper advertising. Since Philadelphia is given prominent feature in the article, special material is being shipped there. Other towns that receive brief mention along with a plug for the stations are Chicago, Los Angeles, Baltimore, Peoria and San Francisco. This should be an easy one for promotion wherever TV stations have their own version of shock theater.

Roland Depicts the Mad Engineer. While at the Sammy House last week, he was called upon to give some assistance in a problem in Physics 40. He is shown busily engaged in solving the problem.

Roland to Visit West Jersey Horse Show

Roland, the TV master of ceremonies of Horrorland, will be one of the feature attractions at the West Jersey Hospital Horse Show to be held June 5, 6 and 7 at Garden State Park. Roland will make his appearance from 3 to 5 p. m. on Saturday, June 7.

* * *

A display of 32 antique automobiles will parade as one of the many features planned for the 20th annual West Jersey Hospital Horse Show to be held at Garden State Park Thursday, Friday and Saturday, June 5, 6 and 7.

This novel event is in keeping with the current year's theme, "Down Memory Lane." The parade is scheduled for Saturday at 2 p. m. This phase of the show is under the auspices of the Horseless Carriage Club of Trenton and the North Shore Antique Auto Club of Point Pleasant. Mr. and Mrs. James F. Pardee, of Collingswood, are chairmen of this colorful feature.

Another feature which is new this year, and of particular interest to ladies attending the affair, will be three separate fashion shows.

A maternity show on Friday at 8 p. m. will be presented by the Hessert Shop, Haddonfield, with professional models. Mrs. Clarence J. Eichel, Haddonfield, is chairman of maternity fashions.

Dewees of Haddonfield will present a tots' fashion show Saturday at 10 a. m., under the chairmanship of Mrs. Fred Balint, Haddon Heights.

The Lillian Albus Fashion show will be presented Saturday at 1.30 p. m. on the terrace, followed by a card party. No reservations are required and there is no additional charge to be made for any of the shows or the card party. Mrs. Walter G. Munns, Barrington, is chairman of this fashion show, and Mrs. Harold B. Evans, Haddonfield, is card party chairman.

WEEKLY RETROSPECT – COLLINGSWOOD, N.J.
THURS. MAY 29, 1958

DELAWARE TO

1958
DELAWARE TOWNSHIP NEWS
THURS JUNE 5

'Cool Ghoul' Roland Is West Jersey Show Extra

Roland, the "cool-ghoul" of TV fame, will be an added attraction at the 20th Annual West Jersey Hospital Horse Show at Garden State Park which begins today, June 5, and continues through Saturday, June 7.

The horror movie M.C. will arrive here from Transylvania for Saturday's awarding of trophies at 3 p.m. and will autograph his photograph until 5 p.m.

Tonight's feature attraction will be a teen-age dance from 8 to 10 p.m. with a surprise guest artist. Meals will be served in the cafeteria dining room from 5 to 7 p.m., and a snack bar will open from 7 to 11 p.m.

Many other special events will be under the direction of Mrs. Harrison Todd, of Haddonfield. The food committee, which will also serve a complete hot dinner Saturday evening for $2, is headed by Mrs. William H. Morrison, of Collingswood.

Schedule Of Events

The following is a schedule of events for the three-day benefit show:

Art Exhibit by Prof. Vincenzo Pezzella, charcoal portraits, June 5-6-7, all day.

Nine-hole Golf Course, June 5-6-7, noon to closing.

Teen-age Dance in the Colonial Room, music by the Imperials, tonight, June 5, 8-10 p.m.

Palmist, Horses and Pony Rides, Antique Auto Rides, June 6-7, noon to closing.

Maternity Fashion Show, June 6, at 8 p.m.

Shows For Saturday

Saturday's features include: Dewees Tots Fashion Show at 10 a.m.; Puppet Show, "The Polka Dot Pony" in the Big Top, all day; Fashion Show in the Terrace Room followed by a card party, 1:30 p.m.; and an Antique Auto Parade at ringside, 2 p.m.

Also, presentation of trophies by Roland at ringside at 3 p.m.; Dog and Pigeon Show, 3:30 p.m.; Exhibitors' Reception with Dr. and Mrs. Stanley L. Brown, Dr. an' Mrs. Henry Tatem and Dr. a' Mrs. Robert N. Bowen hostin' to 5 p.m.

West Jersey Hospital

HORSE SHOW AND FAIR

GARDEN STATE
RACE TRACK

JUNE
5, 6 & 7, 1958

I'LL BE THERE . . . YOU BETTER COME and SEE ME

Roland

Other Special Events . . .
- Antique Auto Show
- Horse & Pony Rides
- Miniature Golf Course
- Puppet Show in "The Big Top", etc.

Pointers, Caulkers and Cleaners' Local No. 35, Pa.
B. M. & P. I. U. OF A. — A. F. OF L.
128 W. MONTGOMERY AVENUE
PHILADELPHIA 22, PA.

March 25, 1958

ROLAND
c/o WCAU-TV
Philadelphia, Pennsylvania

Dear Sir & Brother:

It has been brought to our attention that on Saturday night March 22, 1958, you mentioned the fact that you were going to sandblast "My Dear".

It is our duty to inform you that sandblasting comes under the jurisdiction of our Local Union. It is, therefore, our priviledge to make you an honorary member, in good standing, of this union. This will entitle you to sandblast any PERSON within the territorial limits of Transylvania.

Enclosed you will find your up to date Building Trades Card.

Fraternally yours,

Henry C. Tronco
Executive Board

Pointers, Caulkers and Cleaners' Local No. 35, Pa.

James Wilkins   George Rossman
William Swain   John Atkinson
William Atkinson   Henry Tronco
Frank O'Donnel

A Realistic, Suspenseful, Gripping New Murder Mystery!

AN NTA
TV FILM RELEASE

BRAND NEW
NEVER SHOWN
IN THEATERS

THE KEY TO MURDER

Filmed in
Color
Especially for
Television
Under RCA TV
Color Standards

RELEASED THRU
NATIONAL TELEFILM
ASSOCIATES, INC.

Running Time 71 minutes

The KEY To MURDER

Cast

Jane Stewart	Lynn Dollar
Lt. Daley	John Zacherle
Sgt. Coleby	Sam Kressen
Carl Johnson	Tom Slaugh
Frank Johnson	Joe Earley
Paul Sinclaire	Ken Chapin
Dr. Miller	John Clayton
Maggie McCarthy	Kate Morris
Charles Morgan	Marvin Stephens

Credits

Screenplay, Production, Direction, Editing	Alexander Wilson
Director of Photography	Michael Levanios
Asst. Cameraman	Richard DeFrenes
Production Manager	Frank Heininger
Sound	Hal McGargle, John Westing
Art Direction	Homer Johnson
Casting	Doris Jacobson
Script Continuity	Maralyn Sinclair

Synopsis

Charles Morgan lay dead in his room in the house of his fiance, Jane Stewart, shot through the chest. No one had heard the shot, although three other people were in the house at the time. His death apparently was an accident, caused by a rifle he was cleaning, which was found beside him. Also the door and window to the room were locked from the inside. To enter the room, it had been necessary for Dr. Miller, who had been summoned by Jane's cousin, Frank Johnson, when he and his father, Carl Johnson, had been unable to wake Morgan, to knock the key out of the lock onto a piece of paper and bring it through to the outside.

Although the rifle, and the locked door indicated an accident, Dr. Miller insisted on notifying the police. He did this, despite the objections of Frank Johnson, who it develops, was worried about what the police might think if they should discover that he owed Morgan a large sum of money which he had borrowed to cover a gambling debt.

On their first visit, Lt. Daley and Sgt. Coleby, the officers assigned to the case, are convinced that the shooting was an accident, but as a matter of routine, they insist upon an autopsy. The results of this autopsy change the case completely. It reveals that Morgan was shot, not by the rifle beside him, but by a 45 revolver.

Daley and Coleby rush back to the Johnsons', but they are too late to discover that Frank Johnson, during their absence has found the note he gave Morgan and destroyed it.

Their investigation this time, however, reveals that Morgan had another potential enemy. He is Paul Sinclaire, a young writer, who continued to press for Jane's hand even after her engagement to Morgan. He had, in fact, been in the house on the night of the shooting, but had left about two hours before, although no one had actually seen him leave. By piecing together various information about the position of the chain-bolt on the front door, which was confirmed by the maid, Maggie McCarthy, and the cab driver who had brought Johnson home early that morning, Daley and Coleby conclude that Sinclaire couldn't have left until after the time of the murder. They decide to send out an order for his arrest, when to their surprise, he arrives at the house, and is arrested, although maintaining his innocence.

His story is believed by no one, except Jane, who seems more interested in securing his release than in who shot her fiance. Since she is the beneficiary of Morgan's will, this leads Coleby to suspect that she and Sinclaire might have planned the murder together. Daley discounts this possibility, however, as Jane has a large income from a trust fund held by her uncle, Carl Johnson.

Daley and Coleby believe their case to be complete when they find the murder gun and trace it's ownership to Sinclaire. He finally admits it was his gun, but insists he pawned it before the murder. The District Attorney, however, points out that unless they can show how it was possible for Sinclaire to leave the murder room, when it was locked from the inside, there is a good chance that he might be acquitted, since he could not be placed at the scene of the murder.

To close this last link in the chain of evidence against the murderer, Daley asks all the people connected with the case to come to the house for the purpose of re-enacting the various incidents to the crime. During the re-enactment, the real murderer reveals himself, and Jane, who had been engaged to Morgan chiefly to please her family, is re-united with Paul.

ZACH: "The Key to Murder *was a movie made for about $6000. It featured a lot of people from the* Action in the Afternoon *TV show. The idea was to have it get on TV, but I don't think it ever made it. We were cutting corners like crazy. One set was built with flats, like on a stage, very flimsy. When that scene was over, they tore off the wallpaper to reveal different wallpaper underneath it. That's how they changed sets! We tried hard to get it done very quickly in the studio they had rented. It may not have led to anything, but I can't say we didn't enjoy doing it."*

HI GRUESOME!—Roland of television's Shock Theater takes a break from his autograph signing in Wenzel's Auditorium, Tamaqua, to discuss the lighter things in life with Misses Ann Kehoe, (left) and Eleanor Furey, both of Coaldale, members of the sponsoring Panther Valley Spartans Basketball team. Roland appeared before more than 500 youth during a benefit recording dance in Tamaqua for the basketball team.

AUG. 26, 1958
ELPHIA INQUIRER, TU

TV Roundup
Roland Leaves WCAU for Role Of Ghoul in N.Y.

Philadelphia

ROLAND has given notice at WCAU-TV. John Zacherle, who portrays the "cool ghoul," a teen-age favorite hereabouts, is slated to start hosting "Shock Theater" films for ABC's New York outlet, WABC-TV, late next month.

Zacherle's deal with WABC-TV calls for appearances on Friday and Monday evenings.

Zacherle will assume a new name and makeup for his New York stints, but he will remain, he says, "some sort of ghoul."

He's hoping that his new assignment will lead to a network spot. ABC reportedly has been considering several horror series.

There's a possibility that Roland may continue to make local appearances on Saturday evenings.

32   F   **The Evening Bulletin** Tues., August 26, 1958
Channel Chat

THE appearances of Roland, Channel 10's "cool ghoul," will be cut to one night a week — Saturdays — as host of the station's Shock Theater, a spokesman for the station indicated today.

John Zacherle, who plays the role, will expand his eerie activities, however. He has been signed by WABC, the American Broadcasting Company's New York station, to preside over chiller films on Mondays and Friday nights.

The Evening Bulletin Tuesday, Sept. 9, 1958

CHANNEL CHAT

Zacherle Quits as Roland To Take TV Job in N. Y.

JOHN ZACHERLE, who as Roland has been host of Channel 10's Shock Theater, has resigned.

John A. Schneider, general manager of WCAU-TV, in announcing the resignation said Zacherle will cease to be Roland with the Shock program of Saturday, September 13.

Zacherle has signed with WABC-TV New York and is under option to the ABC network. He had previously announced he would host one Channel 10 Shock Theater program weekly instead of two, as he has been doing on Friday and Saturday nights.

"All of us are delighted that our program was the means of Zacherle starting on his new career and we wish him well in his new undertaking," Schneider said. "Shock Theater will continue to be programmed on Friday and Saturdays."

Of all the "cool ghouls," from coast-to-coast who came to prominence with the showing of old Hollywood horror films, Zacherle, as Roland, seems to have made the biggest national impression. WABC New York has announced that it will retain Zacherle under his name "Zacherle," instead of Roland.

NBC will telecast a total of 11

collegiate football games approved by the National Collegiate Athletic Association, starting with the Missouri-Vanderbilt tussle on September 20.

Grid powers from all sections and several classic rivalries, including the annual Army-Navy battle from Municipal Stadium and the 65th annual Texas-Texas A. & M. contest, are scheduled. The network will also carry the Iowa-Notre Dame game on November 22.

Two Big Ten tilts are to be carried on October 4 and October 11, but they have not been selected. Another contest that is apt to be action-packed is the Auburn - Tennessee match on September 27. Lindsey Nelson and Red Grange will again handle commentary for the series.

TO PLACE a "Person to Person" Want Ad in The Bulletin, phone EVergreen 2-7000.

CHANNEL CHAT

Zacherle Quits as Roland

JOHN ZACHERLE, Channel 10's Roland, has quit his "cool ghoul" job, effective immediately, the station disclosed today. Zacherle reportedly was unhappy over his salary. The station said the Roland character will continue on Shock Theater, however, with a new actor in the role. The program is aired Friday and Saturday night at 11.25.

Roland has become a popular character with the teen age set. He has made numerous personal appearances at fraternity dances.

Under his own name, Zacherle recorded "Dinner with Drac," which hit the best-seller charts.

• • •

MILTON BERLE was not the culprit responsible for Tuesday night's Emmy awards show running out of time, NBC said

today. When he came on at 10.32 the show was already 16 minutes late due to every segment running overtime. Uncle Miltie had been allotted seven minutes, took eight and a half, while another minute was consumed by unexpected applause.

• • •

"THE Green Pastures" will be repeated on TV, but not until late next season. The Peabody Award winner will be the Easter presentation of the Hallmark Hall of Fame series.

ZACHERLEY

Good Night, Sweet Demon

Roland in a ghoulish mood.

Shock Theater films in New York. He took it. Roland, actually a gentle young fellow named John Zacherle, uses his own name in his new post, but he is as appalling as ever, and he says, "I hope with my new fiendishness to effect a better understanding between men and monsters." Among his Philadelphia mourners are thousands of teenagers—several children of Post editors are bitterly accusing this magazine of bringing about the loss of their cool ghoul.

In Philadelphia many people are sad because a fiendishly horrible ghoul recently left town. This fearful creep, named Roland (accent on second syllable), introduced and often interrupted the horror movies on station WCAU-TV; he had delightful habits, like keeping his wife, My Dear, staked inside a coffin. Well, right after Roland was featured in a Post article on August sixteenth (TV's MIDNIGHT MADNESS by **Roul Tunley**) he was offered the job of haunting WABC-TV's

Now available on Shock Theater, WABC-TV, CHANNEL 7, New York

The Saturday Evening
POST
October 18, 1958

3

ZACHERLEY
WABC

WHEN THE "SHOCK!" MOVIES BEGAN RUNNING ON NEW YORK CITY'S WABC CHANNEL 7, THERE WAS NO HOST: ALL THAT WAS ADDED TO THE MIDNIGHT MADNESS WAS AN OFFSCREEN STATION ANNOUNCER WITH A CREEPY VOICE, DELIVERING BAD PUNS. (EXAMPLE: "THIS STORY IS ABOUT A MAN MADE MONSTER WHO THRIVES ON ELECTRICITY. *SHOCKING?* OF COURSE!") BUT THEN IN THE SUMMER OF '58, RUMORS STARTED CIRCULATING THAT PHILADELPHIA'S ROLAND HAD BEEN RE-CHRISTENED "ZACHERLEY" AND WAS ON HIS WAY TO WABC TO HOST THE SECOND SEASON OF FRIGHT FILMS.

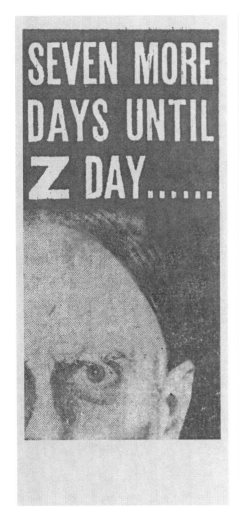

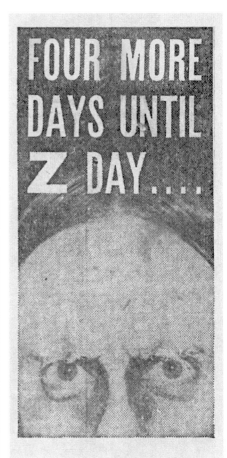

New York Journal-American
26·Wed., Sept. 17, 1958 ★★★★

TODAY IS Z-DAY!

FOR THE FIRST TIME ON TV...

MEET ZACHERLEY YOUR NEW, GHOULISH HOST ON...

SHOCK THEATER
11:15 TONIGHT
WABC-TV CHANNEL **7**

Watch **THE 'MYSTERY' OF EDWIN DROOD**
featuring Claude Rains as a suitor consumed by jealousy

RECIPE FOR GHOULASH. John Zacherle, a professional TV ghoul, demonstrates how he mixes up horror and mayhem in his weird laboratory. Zacherle begins tonight as host on the Channel 7 "Shock Theater." He will add his own special touch to the program's regular horror films.

TV 'Ghoul' Zacherle H(a)unts Sponsors

Even a ghoul has to have sponsors if he wants to go on television.

So, like other TV personalities, a TV-bound ghoul named John Zacherle made the rounds of Madison Ave. the other day in an effort to win friends and influence people. There were screams and stares up and down the avenue as Zacherle—in his own quiet way—went about his work.

He had a whole suitcase full of gory "hands" and he made friends by giving them as gifts. Before long, even the pretty secretaries flocked about him—proving that looks aren't everything. He told them how he was going to be (g)host of WABC-TV's "Shock Theater" on Mondays and Fridays (11:15 PM) starting tonight, and about his lovely subterranean TV laboratory, equipped with work slab, coffins and things of that sort. And he got his sponsor.

Actually, he's a pleasant fellow, whose ghoulish characterizations on a Philadelphia TV station won him a nationwide reputation. About 90,000 persons turned out to see him at a recent stadium rally there. He said that he might eventually hold similar rallies at the now-deserted, haunted Ebbets Field and the Polo Ground.

HAND-SOME HORROR. Ghoul John Zacherle comes to grips with startled ad-agency clerk Dorothy Gless, above, and then finds himself fingered by his own monstrous gag below by agency TV director Ed Fleri.

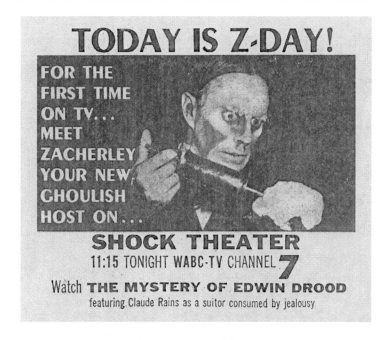

MR. ZACHERLE GOES TO TOWN:

JOHN ZACHERLE KNEW THAT HIS SUCCESS AS ROLAND HAD CAUGHT THE ATTENTION OF TV STATIONS IN NEW YORK. HE MADE A WOMAN NAMED ISOBEL BAKER HIS AGENT AND PROVIDED HER WITH A 20-MINUTE ROLAND KINESCOPE. ISOBEL GOT TV PRODUCER ELLIS SARD INTERESTED, AND NOW HE JOINED IN THE EFFORTS TO PEDDLE ZACH IN NEW YORK. (FOR ALL THE DETAILS, SEE ZACH'S SEVEN-PAGE TYPEWRITTEN "JOURNAL" BEGINNING ON PAGE 123.) ZACH SIGNED A WABC CONTRACT IN AUGUST 1958, AND ON SEPTEMBER 22 HE MADE HIS FIRST NEW YORK APPEARANCE, HOSTING THE 1935 CHILLER *MYSTERY OF EDWIN DROOD.* THE WABC SERIES FEATURED TWO NEW CHARACTERS, BOTH UNSEEN: GASPORT (A CREATURE IN A POTATO SACK) AND ASSISTANT JANOS. AND ZACH'S COFFIN-BOUND WIFE "MY DEAR" NOW HAD A NAME: ISOBEL (NAMED FOR ISOBEL BAKER).

CLEARING THE CHANNELS

It's a Lonely Town, Roland Says of N.Y.

By HARRY S. GLOVER
Staff Writer

Remember old Roland, the fellow who was so popular hereabouts as WCAU-TV's cool ghoul on the late movie show?

Roland's been over in New York for four months under a different name but using the same format that was so successful on Channel 10. He breaks into late-at-night horror films (horrors in more ways than one) with his sticking-plaster hairdo, pallbearer's getup and fusty line of gab.

From a conversation I had recently with Roland, or John Zacherle, to give him his real name, I gather the old boy isn't altogether happy in New York.

"The show is going quite well," Zacherle said, **"but I have a pretty lonely life of it in New York. It's a strange city."**

Being cooped up in a hotel room, he indicated, is not a very satisfying mode of existence. And he doesn't care for the constant noise that is an ingrained part of New York living. The endless honking of taxicabs fighting the battle of crosstown traffic, the rapping of an air hammer as it bites a piece out of the street — these and other sounds may be music to the hardened ears of a veteran New Yorker but not to Zacherle's.

The old WCAU-TV favorite said he doesn't get much chance to go out and hit the spots in Jugtown because of his hours. He's on at 11:15 p.m., just about the time things are beginning to warm up.

'Breathes Again'

"Every weekend when I'm off I go back to my home in Flourtown (Montgomery County)," Zacherle told me. "My mother lives there. I still keep most of my things there. It gives me a chance to breathe again."

Zacherle's station is WABC-TV, Channel 7. He appears visually on the station's "Shock Theater" Mondays and Fridays, the rest of the week he's heard but not seen.

Zacherle, whose name for some reason is spelled Zacher-

ley on the New York show, has some new creatures with him.

Instead of his "My Dear" of the Channel 10 days, he now has a "wife" named Isabel, who plays gruesome tunes on a tiny piano in her coffin-like hideaway.

In place of the invisible Igor, known and loved by old Roland fans, Zacherle now sports a character he calls Gastort. "I also refer to him as my 'burlap boy,' because I keep him stowed away in a burlap bag."

Another of Zacherle's phantom pals is Yanoush, who wanders around the studio haunting everybody from the producer down to the guy who brings in salami sandwiches. Yanoush, it is suspected, is a former TV time salesman who in a moment of pique dashed westbound into the eastbound exit of the Holland Tunnel.

Cool to Hour

Zacherle revealed his principal reason for leaving WCAU-TV last September to go to New York.

"They wanted to move me

from the 11:15 late movie back to the 12:45 late, late movie," he said. "I didn't think I would get as big an audience at that hour — too many people would be in bed by quarter of one in the morning. So I left.

Zacherle said the wheels in New York have been discussing the idea of having him go network. But nothing has jelled yet.

Washington was admitted to the Union on Nov. 11, 1889.

11:00—
11:30—Cɔ.
P.M.
12:00—Tic Ta.
12:30—It Could ᴸ.
1:00—Award Thea.
2:00—Truth or Conse.
quences
2:30—Haggis Baggis
3:00—Young Doctor
Malone
3:30—From These Roots
4:00—Queen for a Day
4:30—County Fair
5:00—In Sherwood
Forest
5:30—Roy Rogers
6:00—Men of Annapolis
6:30—Pulse of the News
6:40—Weather
6:45—News
7:00—Jim Bowie
7:30—Northwest Passage
8:00—Ellery Queen
9:00—M Squad
9:30—Thin Man
10:00—East-West Pro
Basketball
11:00—Vince Leonard
11:10—Weather
11:15—Jack Paar
A.M.
1:00—Science Fiction
1:30—News
1:35—Thought for Tomorrow

1:3.
2:00—ᴸ.
2:30—Mua.
3:00—Beat th.
3:30—Bandstand
5:30—Mickey Mo
6:00—Popeye Th.
7:00—Newsreel
7:10—Weather
7:15—Don Godda
7:30—Rin Tin Ti
8:00—Walt Disne
9:00—Man With
Camera
9:30—77 Sunset
10:30—Newsreel
10:40—Weather
10:45—John Daly
11:00—World's Be.
Movies
A.M.
2:05—All Night S

From the desk of --
                Barbara Haddox

TO: "Zach"

I continue to be ever so
proud of you - it looks
like you really have it
made!

Of what I hear from Phila.,
things are still in a mess
at the station and people
continue to be leaving -
Bud Vaden's gone with
Westinghouse in Baltimore.

                Bestest,

                Barb

ABOVE: *Once Zach hit it big in New York, he received this note of congratulations from a past WCAU co-worker.*

FACING PAGE: *In this winter 1958 interview, Zach makes the comment, "I have a pretty lonely life of it in New York. It's a strange city." Today he can't believe he said that. Zach: "I don't know why I said that. That's what I said? Well, I deny it! I thought New York was a wonderful place. It still is. Maybe I saw some lonely people who looked strange [laughs]."*

MAN FROM TRANSYLVANIA

While the name Zacherley probably means naught to most older folks, there are some young angry young men (and women) who are quite taken up with the antics of the gentleman from Transylvania. He appears weekends after 11 p.m. on ABC-TV and generally speaking, his programs are a farce.. They are centered on an old "horror" film, and by that we mean old, most of them not classified by the Legion of Decency because they were made before 1935.

The movies are to be laughed at rather than cringed at, and this the mc, attired appropriately in black with an unusual hair do, does quite often. In fact high spots of the program are his being dubbed in as one of the crowd in perennial chase of Frankenstein, or as one of the figures in the inevitable wax museum as the killer prowls about. All in all Zacherley, to the people to whom he is directed, presented as it is at a late hour, is an above-average spoof on the old-line Hollywood were-wolf-monster type productions. With his "vampire" wife Isabelle and son Gasport (and old bag hanging on the wall) he is more laughable than believable.

Yet a recent regrettable incident occurred in Jersey City which calls for censorship. A 12-year-old boy told inquiring police that he and five other boys went on a "horror" kick after forming a Zacherley club. They went to Holy Name Cemetery broke into a mausoleum and stole a skull for use in their clubhouse. There they set it up on a pedestal flanked by lighted candles, "to make things more realistic." Their clubroom contained among other objects a makeshift coffin, pictures of monsters, knives, bottle marked poison and sign inviting people to "come in and talk with Zacherley."

Our suggestion of censorship in this instance is not directed at the program but at the parents of the 12-year-old and the other gang members, who included two boys six years old What are they doing up after 11 p.m. and past midnight watching this program? Don't the parents check to see where their boys go when they hold their meetings? It would seem that the delinquency in this case is not juvenile.

ZACHERLEY

Now available on Shock Theater, WABC-TV, CHANNEL 7

Journal NEW YORK American —PICTORIAL TView. SUNDAY, DECEMBER 14, 1958

PREPARING A POTENT POTION, Zacherley, host of TV's Shock Theatre, works with the diabolical tools of his trade.

WITHOUT MAKEUP, Zacherley is a slim, pleasant-looking chap.

FIEND With A Sense of Humor

By Harold Bender

ZACHERLEY, THE DRACULA-like host of WABC-TV's Shock Theatre, reveals he has received several proposals of marriage from distaff horror fans. "They must be all mad," he says. But if the many Shock clubs which have sprouted like toadstools in a werewolf's cave are any indication, a considerable number of vicarious friends are mad about TV's garrulous ghoul.

We came face to face with the monster wit and were not frightened into even one goose pimple. Without his working costume, Zacherley (real name John Zacherle) is tall and slim, is soft-spoken and makes a diffident appearance. He probably would be overlooked in the Madison Avenue crowd and he prefers it that way.

In speaking of his show, he says there is an attempt at satire but the usual effect is slapstick. "We try to kid the daylights out of the film," he says. To accomplish this, Zacherley has created a character who is dressed to kill—a fiend that is inept but with a sense of humor. He is constantly injecting himself into the movie with his role played strictly for laughs. During a scene in a dull monster movie one of the performers pointed to an unseen museum display saying: "That would be ideal for keeping my wife in line." The camera switched to Zacherley hawking a handful of wriggling snakes.

"The first night I interrupted the film, several viewers telephoned to complain that some idiot was sticking his face into the movie," he recalls.

As an aid to relieving horror tension, Zacherley tries to duplicate the experiments of the film monsters, and he has performed brain operations on cabbages, given courses in mummy wrapping and demonstrated the lost art of preparing spider soup. All end in failure. Yes, even ghouls have their real-life troubles. "We've had so many explosions on the show the engineers have threatened to walk out," he says sadly. This threat has compelled Zacherley to curtail some of his more drastic experiments, but he still manages to have butter-fingers with a bottle of nitro-glycerine or a bagful of black widow spiders.

Putting life and humor into the horror films that were popular during the 30's and 40's is deadly serious business. Zacherley and Ellis Sard, Shock Theatre's co-producer and writer, watch the movies for hours to determine the ideal places to cut in for the humorous effect. Though a sort of script is prepared, it does not straight-jacket

STRICTLY FOR LAUGHS, TV's fiend prepares brain for operation.

Zacherley. "I couldn't work that way," he says.

The host's prime objective is to entertain and even commercials get their share of the Zacherley treatment. During an experiment in outer space, Zacherley was eagerly awaiting a message from Mars and received several commercials, instead. After they had run their course, he angrily asked: "Who was jamming the message." He's also referred to commercials as infuriating interruptions.

The unorthodox performer confesses he became an actor because "I'm too lazy to do anything else." Buttressing his claim that he is not overly ambitious, he cites the fact that at age 39 he finally decided to crash New York television. He had been content to make his way professionally in his native Philadelphia, where he would have remained but for the likes of Dracula and Frankenstein.

A graduate of University of Pennsylvania, he spent five years in the U. S. Army and served in Europe and Africa during World War II. Following his discharge, he decided to become an actor as "working nine to five in an office did not appeal to me."

After jobs as announcer and actor on radio in Philadelphia, he broadened his background with several seasons in summer stock with a Chestnut Hill, Pa., theatre group—the Stagecrafters. His big break arrived in 1954 when he became a regular member of the cast of Action in the Afternoon, a TV western serial done live which originated in his hometown.

"I did character parts," he reveals. "One of my roles was that of an undertaker. The TV station's vice president remembered it, and he picked me to do the Shock character for the local horror movie show without an audition."

Hired as host of Philadelphia's Macabre Show in October, 1957, Zacherley transfused new life into the staid City of Brotherly Love. An announcement on the air that his "wife" needed human hair for a new pillow for her coffin resulted in an avalanche of 23,000 letters with hair of assorted colors. More than 800 Zacherley fan clubs were formed. His recording of Dinner With Drac sold over 250,000 discs.

Though on TV he refers to his wife, the woman he met in the basement of Count Dracula's castle in Transylvania, Zacherley is a bachelor. He considers his life to be too leisurely for a woman to want to enter it.

He has been host of Shock Theatre since last September. Though the films are shown six nights a week—at 11 p. m. Monday thru Friday and 10:30 p. m. on Saturday—he is on camera only on Monday and Friday and is heard but not seen the other nights. His off-screen time is spent in devising experiments for future shows, tending his garden and trying to get in an occasional 18 holes of golf.

Zacherley, who was cloaked in anonymity for so long, is taking his success calmly. He continues to commute from Philadelphia where he lives with his mother. He looks back at last Summer somewhat wistfully, regretting that his new-found fame prevented him from playing even one round of golf.

"Where did the Summer go?" he inquires as if he lost a dear friend.

He refuses to make any plans for the future except "to stay with the Zacherley character as long as I can." Another dreaded TV monster—rating services—will determine that.

ZACHERLEY

Now available on Shock Theater, WABC-TV, CHANNEL 7

NEW YORK HERALD TRIBUNE, FRIDAY, SEPTEMBER 26, 1958

Radio and TV: The New 'Shock' Comics

Marie Torre Reports

Funnier, Wilder Than Gleason Gag

Television preoccupation with horror movies ("Shock Theater," "Son of Shock," "Shockorama," "Weird Theater," "Not for Nervous People Theater") is developing a curious breed of performer, the ghoulish emcee—or curator, as they're called in them there screamers.

Station managers look to "curators" to raise the hair, blood pressure and pulse of the television audience, in the event the movies alone don't generate a shiver, but in reality they represent a worthier cause. They're the new hope of TV comedy.

Next time somebody asks, "Where are tomorrow's comedians coming from?" we're going to suggest he look in on the curators because their characterizations are funnier and wilder than anything Jackie Gleason ever invented.

That creature called Zacherley, who works out of a subterranean laboratory at ABC on Monday and Friday nights, is a case in point.

Went Over Big in Philly

In Philadelphia, where he used to perform his macabre rituals until ABC lured him to New York last week, Zacherley consistently outrated Jack Paar ("Poor Jack, he was never any trouble to me"). The Philadelphians found Zacherley —real name, John Zacherle—such a card that they regularly invited him to dinners and dances and various other functions for the purpose of making them laugh.

"It was a revelation to me," said Zacherle, a tall, slender, unassuming forty-year-old, who looks like any advertising man on the 5:07 to Westport when the monster makeup is removed. "I'm an actor basically, have been since the end of the war. I never imagined myself a comedian, but I seem to be now. I even had to prepare some routines for those appearances off television. It's not clown stuff, you know. Mostly sarcastic talk. Straight insult sort of thing. People, I guess, like to be told they're goofy."

Even Dick Clark, idol of the teenagers, invited Zacherle to share his TV camera after the latter's recording, "Dinner With Drac" found its way to jukeboxes. "Clark asked me to go on his show because he said the kids were 'bugging' him to put me on. I had to change the 'Dinner With Drac' lyrics for the appearance, though. Clark thought they were a little too ghoulish for network exposure. The lines about mummy's veins were changed to straws from a witch's broom."

Besides introducing the films on "Shock Theater," Zacherle's specialty is to intrude on the movies occasion-ally to heighten the fright. During a supper scene in Dracula's tomb, for instance, Zacherle is cut in to give the effect he's actually at the supper—a situation which, needless to say, offers unlimited opportunity for ghostly—or ghastly—conversation.

"The whole idea," says Zacherle, "is to spoof the horror films. It's really good fun. If we get very successful with this, maybe I'll get a 'wife' eventually and do a Honeymooners series for TV. Charles Addams' type of honeymooners, of course."

In real life, Zacherle doesn't have a wife. He never earned enough as an actor to

Zacherley   Zacherle

afford one and now that he can afford matrimony he wonders if "it's too late." Somehow, he seems content, both personally and professionally. He doesn't happen to be one of those actors with a burning ambition to play "Hamlet."

"No, I have no interest in playing 'Hamlet,'" he said emphatically, "not unless I can play it in Zacherley attire."

Was that Shakespeare rumbling in his grave we just heard?

*   *   *

Marie Torre

TV-RADIO

Eric Sevareid Explains

"I've been at CBS for twenty years with almost no leaves. It's a pretty grinding job, sometimes working seven days a week... I've gotten awfully stale and I want to get away for awhile. Really, there's nothing behind it."

The words had a familiar Murrowesque ring but this time it wasn't Edward R.; the speaker was Murrow's longtime side-kick and another of CBS's top-ranking newsmen, Eric Sevareid. He let it be known that, as of June 1, he would depart his Washington beat for a four-month leave of absence. Sevareid insisted, however, that he had every intention of returning to the network sometime next fall, on special assignment to the London bureau.

"I was afraid people would think there was some connection between my leave and Ed Murrow's," said the veteran commentator, who has a reputation for independence the equal of his colleague's. "But there just isn't. This isn't part of a general move out of CBS, and I don't know of anyone else in the news department who is planning to leave."

Spoofing the Spooks

Of all the "monsters of ceremonies" haunting horror movies on late-night TV across the country, none has proved so diabolically successful as a tall, frock-coated cadaver called simply "Zacherley." As Frankenstein and Dracula films of the '30s are rolled creakily across ABC-TV's New York screen, sepulchrally cynical Zacherley makes laughable hash of the old chillers by getting into the pictures himself.

While young Boris Karloff, Bela Lugosi, and Lon Chaney go on gravely carving people up or transplanting brains, Zacherley—by a switch from film to "live," and back again—appears in their midst and steals the show. He leers, passes the scalpel, pets the dreaded black cat, and even appropriates their best lines with unhelpful hints and little wisecracks. As Frankenstein's monster comes to life for the umpteenth time this week, Zacherley will interject: "You didn't have to go to med school all those years to learn *that,* Doc."

Zacherley's spook-spoofing has tripled the rating of the year-old show. Beginning this week, ABC will give him a better slot (Saturday nights as well as Friday nights) and change the show's title from "Shock Theater" to "Zacherley at Large." The old film chillers will be chopped, too, to give more time to Zach.

Hair: Minus his death's-head make-up, Zacherley is a shy, young-looking 40-year-old bachelor actor from Germantown, Pa. His actual name is

Zacherley: Under the make-up . . .

Graphic House

. . . an ambitious character actor

John Zacherle. He claims he had never seen a horror film in his life until September 1957 when Philadelphia's WCAU, for which he had once played an undertaker on TV, chose him to be "Roland," host of the batch of old horror pictures they had just acquired. To test his popularity after a few months, he asked each viewer to send in three hairs, so that Zacherley's "wife" might have a new pillow in her coffin. To everyone's astonishment, 23,000 letters poured in—69,000 hairs in all, enough to line her coffin and Zach's coffers as well. ABC, impressed by his success in Philadelphia, brought him to New York for its own low-rated "Shock" series last September.

Zacherley has encouraged his teen-age audience to send him hair-raising objects, and has often had his own hair raised by what he gets. "Some of this stuff makes me squirm," he said last week, fondling his latest gift: A brain

with a wild eye and scissors stuck in it. "We have to throw away the real animal brains that sons of butchers send us."

What will happen to Zach when his movies become so mildewed that they are completely unusable? "Well, I like this mad scientist sort of thing I play," he said, and went on to say he hopes to use it in straight character comedy. "But I'll miss these old movies. I must have seen all 72 of them at least eight times and been in most of them three or four times each. Aren't they marvelous? They all have the same plot whether it's apes, mummies, werewolves, or monsters. Most of them even use the same chase scene—budget too low to reshoot, I guess. You know the one—the mob with torches and bloodhounds angrily combing the marsh and hillside. I'm sometimes afraid they'll do it to ABC—can't you see them coming up through Central Park right now?"

Now the 'Talk' Jockey

The music, music, music formula has long dominated America's highly prosperous local radio stations. Last week in Portland, Ore., radio station KLIQ had pulled a switch to talk, talk, talk, twelve hours a day, six days a week.

The reason for the startling turnabout: Station manager Dick Calender, anxious to make his 1,000-watter unique, had observed that seven out of the ten top-rated radio programs in the Portland area were news shows. So he supplanted the station's three disk jockeys with four staff announcers and numerous taped "correspondents." In a struggle to avoid monotony he made a rule that no voice was allowed more than six consecutive minutes on the air.

On KLIQ there is no set order for the segments, which deal with everything from headline news to advice to the lovelorn. A typical half hour will begin with one voice giving the headlines of the day, then another reading weather and radio reports, still another switching to Washington for political commentary, followed perhaps by a canned interview with a traveler who has recently returned from Japan (telling about the growth of Oriental supermarkets), and then a series of telephone interviews with listeners, asking, for example, "What do you think of socialized medicine?"

Only the weather, which in meteorologically undependable Portland is a matter of primary concern, can be depended on: It's reported at regular fifteen-minute intervals.

"What could be duller than listening to the same top 40 tunes day after day?" Calender asks. So far, listeners seem enthusiastic, and the advertisers have remained loyal. This doesn't particularly surprise Calender: "The musical commercials stand out. They really sing when surrounded by talk."

American Broadcasting Company

INTERDEPARTMENT CORRESPONDENCE

To   ALL CONCERNED

From   Tak Kako

Date   November 26, 1958

Subject   SHOCK THEATER

The following features are booked for SHOCK THEATER,
Mondays - Fridays at 11:15 PM; Saturdays 10:30 PM.

Week Of	MON-TUES-WED	THURS-FRI-SAT
12/29	SON OF FRANKENSTEIN Bela Lugosi, Boris Karloff	BEFORE I HANG Boris Karloff, Evelyn Keyes
1/5	MAD GHOUL Turhan Bey, Evelyn Ankers	FACE BEHIND THE MASK Peter Lorre, Evelyn Keyes
1/12	DEAD MAN'S EYES Lon Chaney, Jean Parker	MAN WITH NINE LIVES Boris Karloff, Roger Pryor
1/19	MUMMY'S TOMB Lon Chaney, Turhan Bey	INVISIBLE MAN Claude Rains, Una O'Connor
1/26	THE CAT CREEPS Lois Collier, Paul Kelly	GHOST OF FRANKENSTEIN Lon Chaney, Lionel Atwill
2/2	DRACULA'S DAUGHTER Otto Kreuger, Gloria Holden	THE WOLFMAN Lon Chaney, Ralph Bellamy
2/9	MAN WHO CRIED WOLF Lewis Stone, Barbara Reed	THE MUMMY'S CURSE Lon Chaney, Dennis Moore
2/16	SPIDERWOMAN STRIKES BACK Gale Sondergaard, Kirby Grant	SOUL OF A MONSTER Rose Hobart, Jeanne Bates
2/23	NIGHT MONSTER Bela Lugosi, Lionel Atwill	MAN THEY COULD NOT HANG Boris Karloff, Roger Pryor
3/2	DRACULA Bela Lugosi, David Manners	THE MUMMY Boris Karloff, David Manners
3/9	HOUSE OF HORRORS Bill Goodwin, Robert Lowery	SHEWOLF OF LONDON June Lockhart, Don Porter
3/16	MAN MADE MONSTER Lon Chaney, Lionel Atwill	JUNGLE CAPTIVE Otto Kreuger, Vicky Lane
3/23	WEIRD WOMAN Lon Chaney, Anne Gwynne	THE BLACK CAT Boris Karloff, Bela Lugosi
3/30	DANGER WOMAN Brenda Joyce, Don Porter	BEHIND THE MASK Boris Karloff, Constance Cummings

Booked by   Tak Kako   Approved by   Al Hollander

AFTER I LEFT FOR N.Y.C. A CH 17
PERSON CALLED ME AND ASKEDIF I COULD COME
BACK AND TAPE A SHOW IN THE STUDIOS IN
CHELTENHAM (I BELIEVE), — I HAD TO TURN THEM DOWN
SO THEY HIRED JOE WHO BECAME FAMOUS ON
THIS U.H.F. STATION AS "DOCTOR SHOCK"!

ABOVE: *In this excerpt from a Zach letter to a fan, he reveals how
another TV horror host, Joe Zawislak's "Dr. Shock," got his start.*

TV'S NIGHTMARES (*Continued*)

ZACHERLEY frolics through
films on New York City's WABC-TV

Transylvania's gift to the outside world is Zacherley, gleeful curator on
New York City's *Shock Theatre* (Mon. and Fri., 11:15 P.M., WABC-TV),
a super spoof who's all for organizing the horror hosts around the
country. Chiding his viewers as being sick-sick-sick to be watching the
"sticky" pictures in the first place, Zach gives educational lectures
on mummy wrapping, brain surgery and other topics of import like speaking
his native tongue, for which he uses such phrases as "my mother is in
the quicksand." Zach's a nattily dressed, prankish looking sort of a fellow
with the kind of boyish lovableness usually associated with the late
Wallace Beery. And he's gentle, too. If you doubt that, consider the way
he treats Isobel, the vampire he met, wooed and wed in the basement
of Count Dracula's castle in Transylvania. He feeds her goodies (like live
spiders), loosens the stake in her heart, plays honeymoon bridge
with her. He and Gasport—a creature who lives in a sack—even surprised
her with a birthday party. Zach truly puts himself into his work, showing up
throughout the films—standing graveside at a
funeral, conducting experiments, spying from
an adjoining dungeon, solemnly preparing tanna
leaves for a hungry mummy. In reality he's
actor John Zacherle, a modest, witty and charm-

ing bachelor of 40 who lives in a "quiet crypt" near his subterranean lab at the ABC studios in
Manhattan. Though last September marked his start as Zach, it was not his start as a ghoulie.
For a year he'd been leading the monster rally in his native Philadelphia as Roland. A
University of Pennsylvania graduate, he saw World War II service in Europe and Africa; is a major
in the Army Reserves; acted in stock, radio and afternoon TV before the Roland role, the recording
of *Dinner With Drac* and the New York offer. Doing two different animated shows a week,
announcing *Shock Theatre* three other nights, writing his material and appearing at occasional
school functions keeps John too busy to think of much else except weekend visits with his mother
in Philadelphia, reading and digging in the garden. For all *we* know he may weekend in
Transylvania consulting with "the count" and digging elsewhere! But no matter to his more
than 50,000 card-carrying fan club members who—to use a Zach expression—think he's "grand."

"THE OLD STAND-BY" --with all the original
verses

(To the tune of Sweet Betsy from Pike)

Now this is the story
Of Doc Frankenstein
He made a big monster
And it turned out fine.
Oh, he sewed it together
Each muscle and joint,
And he won a blue ribbon
For his needlepoint!

Count Dracula sleeps in his coffin
all day.
When night is descending
He goes out to play,
Puts on his tuxedo
White shirt underneath
Then he takes out a nail file
And sharpens his teeth!

A young man named Larry
Went walking one night
A werewolf attacked him
And they had a fight
Now Larry goes prowling
With hair on his face
And he doesn't wear shoes
Which is quite a disgrace!

Old Kharis was buried alive
So they say
For three thousand years
In his wrappings he lay
'Cause he loved Ananka
Who's cute as can be,
Now they drink to each other
With tanner leaf tea!

Oh, Dr. Praetorius
Made little men
He made tiny women and
children, and then
Everyone in Visaria
Wanted to go
To see the old Doctor
And his puppet show!

--Cathy Hart

Zacherley fan Audrey Marshall (professional name: Cathy Hart) furnished him with monster-related lyrics to be sung to the tune of old folk songs. Zach used some on his show and one on The Pat Boone Show *(the song shown here). He paid her small writing fees out of his own pocket.*

To Ellis Hand

MR. GORDON KUNZ   January 8, 1959

G. E. Hamilton

I have been advised by Mr. Bourcier that talent on
the Zackery Show is abusing lavalier type microphones.
It is reported that on three separate occasions of recent date,
that microphones have been drenched requiring return to the
manufacturer for repair.

Obviously, this practice cannot be condoned and must be
stopped.

                                                G. E. Hamilton

CC: Al Hollander, Jr.

'Cool Ghoul' invading the Branford

Zacherly

Zacherly, the "cool ghoul" who usually invades living rooms in the dying hours of the day via ABC-TV, will make a rare "live" appearance in the outer world of humans Tuesday on the stage of the Branford Theater at 7:30 and 9:30 p.m.

The frock-coated monster with the cadavar complexion interrupted his luncheon-spider shish-kabob washed down with Dracula fizz—yesterday to report that a highlight of his appearance in Newark will be a wolf-calling contest.

"The winner will be chosen by the audience and will be awarded a prize — 25 cents in cash," Zacherly said sourly.

There will also be a mad dance contest to pick the most miserable dancers in New Jersey.

"Werewolves are invited," the cool ghoul said with a grin.

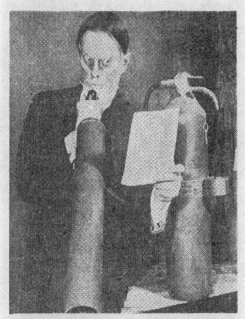

POPULAR GHOUL—A ghoul with a sense of humor, named Zacherley, goes through his monstrous act on WABC-TV's "Shock Theater." As a sort of tongue-in-cheek ghoulish disc jockey, Zacherley has won a large audience in the New York area. He interrupts horror movies with laugh-provoking comments, and even breaks into commercials.—(Wide World Photo)

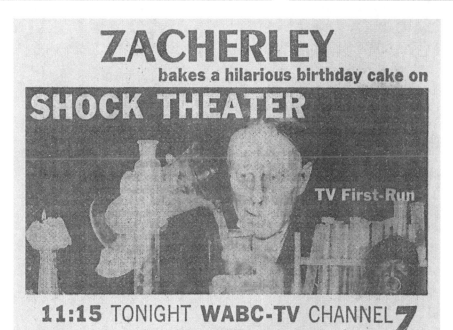

ZACHERLEY
bakes a hilarious birthday cake on
SHOCK THEATER
TV First-Run
11:15 TONIGHT WABC-TV CHANNEL 7
as the Wolf Man, Dracula and Frankenstein rub shoulders in
HOUSE OF FRANKENSTEIN
KARLOFF & LON CHANEY

AMUSEMENTS

Zacherly, TV Star, to Present Horror Show at Capitol Theatre

The New York area's most lovable monster — gruesome, tall and cadaverous looking in his black frock coat, will penetrate the outside world when he appears on stage at the Capitol Theatre, Monroe street, Passaic, on Tuesday evening, August 4 at 8:45 p.m.

This "monster of ceremonies" who haunts horror movies every Friday and Saturday evening on WABC-TV, is a fellow named Zacherly. Beloved by teen-agers and older stay-awakes, he is appropriately known as the "cool ghoul" who performs brain operations and keeps his wife, a vampire named Isobel, safely tucked away in a coffin.

At the Capitol theatre, Zacherly will hold forth amidst a welter of werewolves, mad scientists, plain sadists and a varied assortment of monsters of mayhem and murder. In addition he will present an assortment of gags and hilariously funny frightening experiences to scare the wits out of the audience.

After he invites everyone to sample his favorite brew, "spider soup" the sepulchral appearing Zacherly will conduct a Woolen City wolf calling championship, a crazy dance contest to find the most miserable dancers and other features.

In keeping with the mad, supernatural atmosphere that will prevail at the Capital theatre on Tuesday evening, August 4th, Manager Edward Molteni of the Capitol has announced that he will present a horror movie thriller as the evening's screen fare.

Fans who are brave enough to witness these goings-on and who are followers o fthe Zacherly-at-Large TV program, are urged to purchase their tickets in advance at the Capitol, because indications are that residents from the entire north Jersey area will be in attendance to view the lovable ghoul.

Movie Tim

FABIAN — "Some 1 2:15, 5:35, 7:40, chete," 1:00, 4:20.

GARDEN — "Say O 2:30, 6:00, 9:30; 1:10, 4:40, 8:10.

MEJESTIC — "Fir: Space," 2:20, 6:10, kyo After Dark," 8:25; "Texas City, "Patterson - Johan: 2:00, 5:55, 9:45.

Route 3 Drive-In — The Top," 9:00, 1 Your Blessings,"

Route 46 Drive-In — se James," 8:35, In The Net," 10:3

U.S. — "Shane," 1:0! "Houdini," 3:25, 7

CAPITOL — "Pork 2:00, 5:00, 8:00, 1 fight At Dodge 6:35, 9:40.

CENTRAL — "Say C 1:10, 4:50, 8:35; "G A Hanging," 3:10,

MONTAUK — "So: Hot," 2:10, 5:30, "Machete," 1:00, 4

At the end of 1958 64,750,000 telephones the U.S.

Eddie Hodges Would Like to Be "Like Boris Karloff"

BY HARRY HARRIS

CHILD actors, by general agreement, are mostly monsters. Red-haired, green-eyed Eddie Hodges, 12, isn't—but he wants to be.

He'd like nothing better, he told us, than to portray the Wolf Boy or Frankenstein's Monster.

"I'd like to be like Boris Karloff," he said enthusiastically. "He's my favorite actor. And Lon Chaney, Jr., and Bela Lugosi—wow!

"I get to see horror pictures once in a while. My Daddy sometimes lets me if I have lots of time off before a show, but he gives me the advice of not going because it might affect the show.

"Also, I don't sleep good afterwards, because I stay awake for hours—thinking of how I could do the part!"

One of his fondest memories is the time his friend, hair stylist Grady Bundrick, made him up to look like Frankenstein's Monster for a Halloween Party attended by the cast of Broadway's "The Music Man," in which Eddie appeared 405 times.

"There was a guy there in a Frankenstein mask," he recalled blissfully, "and I looked exactly like him. He had eyes like *this*!" Eddie demonstrated, horrifyingly.

"*Boy!*" said Eddie.

Although his television watching is carefully controlled, Eddie reports he sometimes gets to see New York's "Shock Theater," which stars alumnus-of-Philadelphia TV John ("Roland") Zacherle.

"I'd like to meet him," said Eddie. "Some people say he's a nut, but he looks like a nice man."

We said we considered Zacherle a quiet, retiring sort. "Quiet!" exclaimed Eddie, and went into "Shock Theater" sound-effects—a wailing coyote, a burst of machine gun fire.

Among his prized possessions are a couple of shrunken heads, a miniature guillotine, a Frankenstein mask and his own tonsils, under glass.

However, his interests aren't *all* ghoulish. If he can't land a job as a pint-size nightmare-inducer, he'd be perfectly happy to play a sawed-off cowboy instead.

"I got a horse and saddle in March for my birthday," he said, "and I collect guns and pistols. Sammy Davis, Jr., was on the next set, making 'Porgy and Bess,' when I was acting with Frank Sinatra in 'A Hole in the Head,' and he gave me a holster, a belt and a gun. It's a .22 Colt, but it doesn't have a firing pin and its barrel is plugged up.

"I can draw in 99/100ths of a second.

"It's against the law to shoot here in New York, but I have a .22 rifle back home in Mississippi, and Daddy and I went out for some target practice. He shot all around the target, but I aimed from the hip, like 'The Rifleman,' and made that can jump seven times out of eight!"

Neither spooks nor spurs seem likely to figure in Eddie's show business career for some time yet. A TV veteran since the age of 4 (his TV bow followed his radio debut by almost two and a half years), when he sang "Hey, Good Looking" on a Mobile, Ala., hillbilly show. He's visited viewers' living rooms since then in various guises — as singer, straight actor and quiz show contestant.

Eddie persuaded his parents to "try" New York for a specified period, so he could make the TV rounds. He guested with Jackie Gleason, Jack Paar, Paul Winchell and others; was spotted by a "Name That Tune" scout, split a $25,000 jackpot with John H. Glenn, Jr., one of the six Astronauts recently named to make the first manned space flight; added $32,000 on "The $64,000 Challenge," and made numerous TV appearances afterwards, including an "Omnibus" engagement with Helen Hayes in "Mrs. McThing."

As a singer and dancer, he'll co-star with bewhiskered Burl Ives and other "name" players in CBS' "Holiday, U.S.A.," next week—Wednesday, June 3, at 9 P. M., and he has been at work for some time now on a CBS film series, "The Wonderful World of Little Julius," slated for fall, in which he's teamed with Sam Levene and Gregory Ratoff.

In "Little Julius," he'll portray, suitably enough, a child TV star—"something like me, a strange boy."

"Are you strange?" we asked.

"To me I am," said Eddie.

"Why? Well, the other kids on the block (in Flushing) aren't like me. I never did think about building a hot rod or a wagon until I met those kids. Eddie Fisher, I liked him a lot, he gave me a little car that goes by itself. I rode it in Mississippi, but I never thought of building a hot rod out of boxes and wheels.

"I have a secret. I'm going to try to build a steel robot with a glass dome over its head. I have to draw plans, but I'm going to build a hot rod first.

"I try not to be different. I want to be just like other kids, so they won't think I'm stuck up. I think it's bad to be different just because you're on TV.

"I've seen some people on TV who put on airs, and I hope I'm not like that when I grow up. That's a horrible way to be.

"The boys don't tease me, but once in a while they get me mad. They point at my bike and they say, 'Hey, Eddie, what's the matter with your tire? Are you too cheap to fill it up?' I try to keep my bike nice.

"They ask me if I'm going to be on a show, but they never ask to go along. A lot say they'd like to take over my job, because they think they'd like show business. They would, too. It's a lot of fun!"

His youthful father and mother, John and Sue, and sister Diane, 13, take pains to see that he doesn't get inflated ideas of his own importance. His father, Eddie reported ruefully, believes in old-fashioned corrective punishment with a belt. "If I'm bad, it happens often."

He gets a weekly allowance of $1, "and Daddy deducts once in a while. If I don't keep my room straight, I lose about 15 cents.

"They're trying to teach me to hang up my clothes, but I'm lazy. I'm always tired. It takes me about two hours to get all unstretched."

He always says "sir" and "excuse me" and "thank you," we noticed. He and Diane receive three hours a day of private tutoring in a combination office-classroom in the attic of the Hodges home. "That suits me fine. Six hours a day in school? Uh-uh! Not for me!"

He never suffers from stage fright and can memorize with remarkable speed. But every once in a while, he confessed, he forgets a line on-camera, especially if there are "hard words."

Because of a whole string of such words on a recent Pat Boone show, "I had my toes and my eyes crossed. I had to have something crossed, hoping to get it right." He got it right.

THE PHILADELPHIA INQUIRER, MAY 24, 1959

Did you happen to see this. Forgot to give it to you Sunday

ZACH: "*Eddie and I did meet. He lived right here in New York. Nice kid. We had lunch, that kind of thing. It was really nice to meet him. He was a star, you know? I wonder what ever happened to him.*" (For the record, he's now a mental health counselor in his home state of Mississippi.)

Mrs. Raymond Nunziata
121 Adams Street
Deer Park L.I.

Dear Sirs,

Not to long ago I wrote a letter to your chanel, telling you how much I disliked the Shock Theatre Show since you have put Zacherley on. I use to watch Shock Theatre all the time, I enjoyed it very much. Now since that jerk Zacherley has been on, I can not stand to watch your show.

When I wrote the first letter, I made a mistake. I addressed it to Zacherley. The way I spoke of him and how he has ruined my enjoyment of your show, I hardly expected a return letter like the one enclosed. There is no telling how many people have made the same mistake and received the same stupid letter. Maybe they let it pass, but I could not. I enjoyed watching your show so much, I couldn't help but write this letter, hoping you could take Zacherley off your show so I could enjoy it once more.

Sincerely yours,
Mrs. Raymond Nungiata

Please answer—

ABOVE: *Typed recreation of an unreproduceable handwritten letter from a Zach detractor.*

FACING PAGE: ZACH: *"I did* Shock Theater *live, and halfway through the season they introduced me to the tape machine. From then on, I did the show on tape on Thursday afternoons and they'd air it on the weekend [now retitled* Zacherley at Large]. *That meant my weekends were free and I could go back and forth to Philadelphia and check up on my mother, who was hanging in there, and my brother."*

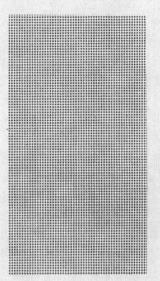

VOL. LIII NO. 14 □ APRIL 6, 1959

Newsweek
THE MAGAZINE OF NEWS SIGNIFICANCE
Titles Registered U. S. Patent Office

—TV-RADIO—

Spoofing the Spooks

Of all the "monsters of ceremonies" haunting horror movies on late-night TV across the country, none has proved so diabolically successful as a tall, frock-coated cadaver called simply "Zacherley." As Frankenstein and Dracula films of the '30s are rolled creakily across ABC-TV's New York screen, sepulchrally cynical Zacherley makes laughable hash of the old chillers by getting into the pictures himself.

While young Boris Karloff, Bela Lugosi, and Lon Chaney go on gravely carving people up or transplanting brains, Zacherley—by a switch from film to "live," and back again—appears in their midst and steals the show. He leers, passes the scalpel, pets the dreaded black cat, and even appropriates their best lines with unhelpful hints and little wisecracks. As Frankenstein's monster comes to life for the umpteenth time this week, Zacherley will interject: "You didn't have to go to med school all those years to learn *that*, Doc."

Zacherley's spook-spoofing has tripled the rating of the year-old show. Beginning this week, ABC will give him a better slot (Saturday nights as well as Friday nights) and change the show's title from "Shock Theater" to "Zacherley at Large." The old film chillers will be chopped, too, to give more time to Zach.

Hair: Minus his death's-head make-up, Zacherley is a shy, young-looking 40-year-old bachelor actor from Germantown, Pa. His actual name is

Zacherley: Under the make-up . . .

Graphic House

. . . an ambitious character actor

John Zacherle. He claims he had never seen a horror film in his life until September 1957 when Philadelphia's WCAU, for which he had once played an undertaker on TV, chose him to be "Roland," host of the batch of old horror pictures they had just acquired. To test his popularity after a few months, he asked each viewer to send in three hairs, so that Zacherley's "wife" might have a new pillow in her coffin. To everyone's astonishment, 23,000 letters poured in—69,000 hairs in all, enough to line her coffin and Zach's coffers as well. ABC, impressed by his success in Philadelphia, brought him to New York for its own low-rated "Shock" series last September.

Zacherley has encouraged his teen-age audience to send him hair-raising objects, and has often had his own hair raised by what he gets. "Some of this stuff makes me squirm," he said last week, fondling his latest gift: A brain with a wild eye and scissors stuck in it. "We have to throw away the real animal brains that sons of butchers send us."

What will happen to Zach when his movies become so mildewed that they are completely unusable? "Well, I like this mad scientist sort of thing I play," he said, and went on to say he hopes to use it in straight character comedy. "But I'll miss these old movies. I must have seen all 72 of them at least eight times and been in most of them three or four times each. Aren't they marvelous? They all have the same plot whether it's apes, mummies, werewolves, or monsters. Most of them even use the same chase scene—budget too low to reshoot, I guess. You know the one—the mob with torches and bloodhounds angrily combing the marsh and hillside. I'm sometimes afraid they'll do it to ABC—can't you see them coming up through Central Park right now?"

ZACHERLEY AT LARGE

FRI. AND SAT. 11:00 PM WABC-TV, CHANNEL 7, NEW YORK

Thursday Dec. 3rd 1959

Television Programs

9 P. M. ⑥ Pat Boone— Everybody's thinking about "Girls, Girls, Girls" on the show tonight. Pat, Eddie Albert, and even that ghoul Zacherley get in the act, so be prepared for Pat and Eddie's "We'll Tell You All About Love," Pat's plaintive "Talk to Me," Zacherley's "My Heart Stood Still," Louise O'Brien's "I Enjoy Being a Girl," and a finale to "Guys and Dolls" from the team of Pat and Eddie. Pleasant.

ZACH: *"Pat Boone was a big fan. My office was near the studio where his show was produced; Pat would wander by and look in my office, which was full of [monster-related] stuff that people would mail in. He would get me invited to his show. Also on the show were some Hollywood people who didn't know who the hell I was [laughs]! He had me on two or three times."*

ZACHERLEY AT LARGE

Dear Whatever You Are:

My ghoulish heart is quickened at the thought
that you have asked to become a member of
WABC-TV's exclusive ZACHERLEY FAN CLUB.

Thank you for being loyal to ZACHERLEY AT LARGE.
We promise the program will continue to live (?)
up to the expectations of its ever-growing
number of ~~fiends~~ friends.

*What the hell do you mean
sending me this rubbish!
I wrote you a letter saying
Zacherley made me swear off
your channel. He is dismal!*

George Kar...

Weirdly,

Zacherley

Zacherley
President

CHANNEL 7 WABC–TV / 7 WEST 66 STREET, NEW YORK 23, NEW YORK

3 May 1959

Dear Howard:

I have enclosed the contract for the Joe Weiss affair.

It seems to me that it would be smart to wait for Harold Cohen's return from the coast before sending this off to Mr. Weiss, because last week there was some serious interest expressed by a contact of Mr. Syd Rubin in doing a series of horror pocket books and there might develope a conflict between the two.

The only thing that worries me about Joe Weiss is that, even though I have expressed myself very definitely on the subject, his forte seems to lean toward the sex and sadism side of the picture. This is something I do not wish to get involved with; there are too many young people in our following. Not that the contract doesn't cover such desires on my part, but I think that he is not capable of writing anything else than what he is used to.

So I would appreciate it if you would hold this paper until I have a chance to talk it over again with Harold... especially in view of the new interest through Mr. Rubin.

Sincerely,

John Z.

Zacherley selected the horror stories for Ballantine's pocket books Zacherley's Midnight Snacks *and* Zacherley's Vulture Stew, *both published in 1960. He had concerns about some of the stories, prompting him to fire off this letter to the publisher.*

48 Saratoga Avenue
Yonkers, New York
June 23, 1959

The A.B.C. Television Company
7 West 66th Street
New York 27, New York.
Dear sir:

WILL YOU PLEASE TELL US IF ZACHERLEY IS COMING
BACK??

PLEASE...

hopefully,
Allen Meyer

Other friends of Zach also hoping:
Cathy Ritagliatta
Roberta Meyer   cont:
Justine Meyer   Richard Little
Joe Hayes   Kurt Zembler
Judy Smolen   Dolly DeVito
Mrs. Diana Wade   Joe Korvette
Anne Rossbach   Martin Walker
Louise Scheldrup   Georgeann Meyer
Jimmy MacDonald   Johnny Bald
Gerildane Bartek   Eillean DiPipo
Sonny Smolen   Jackie Wilson
Joe Bold   and many other Zach's
Lil Brown   fans we don't happen
Phylis Halik   to know, but who
Alf Newman   were no doubt just
Bem Lager   as surprised and
John Worthy   enraged at Zach's
Coley Hawkins   leaving the air.
Marthe McDonough
Murry Linden
Mark Kiphuth
Neil Torstenson
Bill Fiaone
Harry Gonzolla
Joyce Kowsnowski
Jean Brandon
Karen Torstenson
Marty Johnnson
Sol Kurtz
Laura Steele
Lillian McCarthy
Agie Ashburton
John Seaman
Chris Corr
Denis"Dogface" Pett
Bill Elder
John Santos
"Fats" Debinko
Mrs. Hilda Hesch
also;..
Mrs Zacherle (Zach's mom)

When Zach's ABC days came to an end, his followers were not pleased.

4

ZACHERLEY
WOR AND MORE

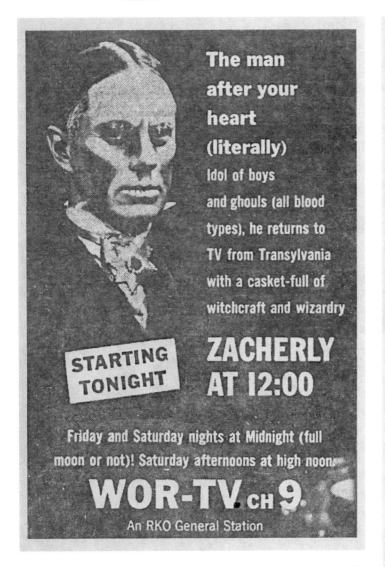

The man after your heart (literally)

Idol of boys and ghouls (all blood types), he returns to TV from Transylvania with a casket-full of witchcraft and wizardry

STARTING TONIGHT

ZACHERLY AT 12:00

Friday and Saturday nights at Midnight (full moon or not)! Saturday afternoons at high noon

WOR-TV. CH 9

An RKO General Station

Don't expect to see Zacherly on Ch. 7 this season. The "mad ghoul" who used to introduce the late-night horror movies on that station has signed with WOR-TV.

Effective Oct. 16, he'll be seen doing the same job on Ch. 9 three times a week — Fridays at midnight and Saturdays at noon and midnight . .

ZACHERLY AT 12
With John Zacherly
Producer: Ray Mulderick
Director: Bob Eberle
WOR-TV, N. Y. (tape)

John Zacherly, the macabre gent introing horror pix, has moved his stand from WABC-TV to the N. Y. RKO Teleradio indic. At his new berth, he remains a suave, ghoulish monster from Cloud Transylvania, adding offbeat, crazy humor to the horror oldies.

Zacherly is slotted at midnight Fridays and Saturdays. With the same taped show played Saturday matinees. He comes in at the opening and closing for from three to five minutes, with unexpected appearances as the feature unrolls.

At the Saturday (24) matinee outing, he was on hand with his wife's coffin on stage. He went through the motions of raising her spirit by feeding her bat milk. Aided by quips and props, his turn was chillingly entertaining. Practice of breaking into the feature, this one starring Boris Karloff and Bela Lugosi, is of questionable value. It may get some kidding laughs, but detracts from the suspense in the film. Some viewers, though, may take the kidding intrusion as their dish of bat milk. In any event, Zacherly is a showmanly addition to horror pix.

NOV. 20   *Horo.*

After ABC, Zach returned to horror-hosting two clicks up the New York dial as the star of WOR Channel 9's Zacherley at 12.

HERALD TRIBUNE INSERT PROOFS

FRIDAY, OCTOBER 30, 1959

TONIGHT—ZACHERLEY MEETS DRACULA ON HALLOWEEN!

Together for the first time since their boyhood days in Transylvania, Zacherley contacts his friend, Count Dracula, in a special graveside interview!

Don't miss this unusual TV first! (It may not happen again for another 100 years)

ZACHERLEY

Tonight at Midnight, Tomorrow at Noon and Midnight

WOR-TV channel 9

An RKO General Station

Tuesday, February 2, 1960   THE BROADCASTER   Page Three

BROADCASTER'S BUZZING ABOUT ...

Royalty in YHS

During a reading of "Macbeth" in Mrs. Daudet's English class, the cast of characters included: Macbeth — William Macbeth, and Duncan — Roger Duncan. Incidentally both Roger and William claim to be descendants of their namesakes.

Les Artists

The creators of that beautiful Christmas mural in Miss Hyra's room were Nick Barberi, Marie Buono, Joan Novotny, and Lorraine Vellozzi.

Kazoo Kazoo

After a long illness, Mr. Abrams has returned to YHS to resume teaching mathematics. On behalf of all his "children", *Broadcaster* extends its heartiest welcome home.

Ikada des ka

Beryl Gorbman is learning to speak Japanese at the Buddhist Temple in preparation for her trip to Japan next year.

Large Charge

Unsuspecting Norman Krasne and Paul Gitelson walked into physics class only to have their sweaters confiscated by Dr. Leitman to use in one of his experiments.

One and a two

The long awaited band uniforms have arrived in time for the dedication ceremony on February 10.

What's A Nice Ghoul Like You Doing In A Place Like This?

In the highly unsophisticated and rather appropriate surroundings of a Greenwich Village cellar, we uncovered WOR-TV's Zacherly.

As Transylvania's chief "Monster of Ceremonies", Zacherly has been conducting a series of enlightening lectures for his T.V. audience. These lectures are liberally laced with gory laboratory experiments which go on in between some "dog" of a movie he is showing.

The cellar heretofore mentioned contained the numerous and for the most part, ghastly entries of his "Draw Isobel" contest. Isobel is his unseen "dear wife" inhabiting a coffin with a loose lid on top.

In reality Zach is charming and mild-mannered John Carson Zacherly, an accomplished character actor. A native Philadelphian, he is a graduate of the University of Pennsylvania (not to be confused with his "Old Country" Transylvania) and commenced ghouling in 1957 as WCAU-TV's rousing Roland. His success led him to New York and Channel 7, and thence to Channel 9, all at the eyerubbing hour of midnight and on. He may be viewed on Channel 9 on the 9 p.m. spot on Tuesdays, Fridays and Sundays.

From time to time, Zach has his Transylvania operas that have recently come into their own. He offers such masterpieces as "The Last Time I Saw Kharis," (a ghoulish affair with an Egyptian flavor), together with "The Student Monster," (not to be confused with the "Student Prince").

Zacherly sternly denied that he is not appearing at the Coconut Grove. This reporter, recalling the macabre genius of a French poet, asked, "Are you a disciple of Beaudelaire?" Impressed by this egghead comment, he drew himself to his ghastly 6'7" and said indignantly, "Disciple! Why, my dear, I taught him everything he knows, of course." Of course...

As the interview drew to a close and the kids unwound themselves from the overhead steam pipes, he was asked the vital question, "Do you take payola?" With a wolfish grin Zacherly answered, "Yest, yes-oh MY yes!"

V-Day Gifts

Miss Meves — A heart-shaped Chinese fortune cookie.

Dr. Leitman — A heart-shaped mercy plea.

Mr. Ross — Mr. Lum's bottle of "No-Doze".

What were the results?
Miss Meves — A stomachache from bad flour.

Dr. Leitman — A good laugh.

Mr. Ross — Was seen hopping and skipping through the halls.

The author — Was kicked off the staff.

Cool

He was cool. First one out on "A" shift, last one in on "B" shift. Sometimes he didn't bother coming in on "B" shift. Life was a drag. He didn't like combination locks. He wasn't overwhelmed by the P. A. system. His homeroom teacher didn't know him. He was cool.

The night before regents was a drag. Regents were for clods. His mother said he was a late-bloomer.

The next day he went to take his French II Regents. He didn't see the sign Latin III on the door. He thought it was a tough regents. He'd write the Board of Regents and tell them what he thought of it. He finished in thirty minutes. He went home to his bongos. He was cool.

GRACIE MANSION

November 1, 1960

Gentlemen:

The Mayor joins me in thanking you for the record "Spook Along with Zacherley", which you were good enough to send us.

We appreciate you thinking of us.

With best wishes,

Sincerely,
Mrs. Robert
(Susan E) Wagner

Zacherley Electra Corp.
116 W. 14th St.
New York, N. Y.

Recreation of a too-light-to-reproduce note Zach received from the wife of New York's mayor.

BRUCE FRIEDMANS THIRD "EFFORT"

THE ZACHERLEY FIASCO

FILM: CONCERNING PRIZE-FIGHTING- IF POSSIBLE

AUDIO: NO THEME !!

IDEA OF SHOW:

IN THE COMING MONTH FLOYD PATTERSON WILL TRY TO REGAIN HIS

TITLE AS THE "HEAVY WEIGHT CHAMPION OF WORLD" FROM THE PRESENT

CHAMPION, INGOMAR JOHANSON. THE PREMIER OF TRANSYLVANIA PREM.

OTRYANT, HAS ARRANGED FOR YOU TO FIGHT THE WINNER OF THIS CONT-

EST, FOR THE CHAMPIONSHIP. IT STANDS TO REASON THAT YOU SHOULD

BEGIN A RIGOROUS TRAINING PROGRAM- TO GET INTO SHAPE FOR THE BIG

FIGHT. TO DO THIS ONE MUST EXERCISE:
SUGGESTED EXERCISES: WEIGHT LIFTING (PHONY WEIGHTS-OF COURSE)
JUMPING ROPE, PUSH UPS, SIT UPS, RUNNING, RIDE BYCICLE ROUND THE
CRYPT..
ISOBEL SUGGESTSTGOING TO VIC TANNA'S HEALTH GYM. IF THE BUDGET

WOULD PERMIT, THIS WOULD BE FINE. BUT THE BUDGET WONT PERMIT....

THE NEXT BEST THING: SINCE YOU'VE SEEN VIC'S ONE MINUTE FILM SO

OFTEN, YOU KNOW HIS WHOLE ROUTINE BY HEART.

JOE YOUNG, HAS VOLUNTERED TO HAVE PRACTICE BOXING MATCHES W/

YOU. (A BOXING RINK COULD BE MADE IN THE CRYPT AREA OR THE CUT*IN

AREA. WITH FOUR CHAIRS AND SOME ROPE.) BY USING STRINGS(AS USUAL)

IT WILL APPEAR THAT JOE IS"ALIVE" AND IS FIGHTING. JOE LOUIS HAD

A VERY DISTINCT STYLE OF FIGHTING..(THE WIDE LEG STANCE AND THE

HANDS HIGH. THIS MIGHT PROVE VERY FUNNY AS YOUR STYLE!)

NOT FORGETTING GASPORT: HE COULD BE STRUNG IN MID CRYPT WITH A

MATRESS ON THE FLOOR..USED AS FOOTBALL PLAYERS USE A SANDBAG DUMMY

TO PRACTICE TACKLING..

PROP LIST: BATHROBE AND TOWEL
           GASPORT AND JOE Y. (STRUNG)
           UNDERSHIRT(NO SLEAVES) W/"T".
           BERMUDA'S FOR REGULAR EXERCISING AND SNEAKERS
           SWIMMING TRUNKS..(BOXER SHORTS WORN UNDERNEATH FOR THE FIGHT!
           WEIGHTS..PHONY'S..
           JUMP ROPE

WOR

1440 BROADWAY, NEW YORK 18
LONGACRE 4-8000

MAY 4 1960

BRUCE FREIDMAN
237 EAST 42nd STREET
BROOKLYN 3, NEWYORK

DEAR BRUCE:

    BY NOW YOU ARE AWARE THAT I FOUND GOOD USE FOR
YOUR TRANSYLVANIAN WEATHER SHOW IDEAS...I THOUGHT
THAT THE LIGHTNING-IN-a-SUITCASE IDEA WAS AS CLEVER
AS THEY COME AND CAME ACROSS IN "GRAND" STYLE AS
I FLOATED HIGH OVER NEW YORK CITY IN OUR WOR BALLOON!

    I SUPPOSE THIS MAY BE YOUR START ON THE ROAD
TO FAME AND FORTUNE...BUT DONT BLAME ME IF YOU ONLY
GET FAMOUS.

                              THANKS AGAIN

                              [signature]
                              JOHN ZACHERLE

R K O   T E L E R A D I O   P I C T U R E S ,   I N C .

WOR, New York - WOR-tv, New York

FACING PAGE: Teenage Zach-oholic Bruce Friedman submitted ideas for *Zacherley at 12* skits; a boxing-related one is described here. Another Friedman suggestion, that Zach explore the stratosphere in a weather balloon, actually made it to the air (pun intended).

T'WAS THE NIGHT BEFORE CHRISTMAS

T'WAS THE NIGHT BEFORE CHRISTMAS
AND ALL THROUGH THE HOUSE
WAS HEARD THE DIRE PREDICTIONS
OF MY PSYCHIC SPOUSE

"YOU MAY HANG YOUR STOCKINGS
BY THE CHIMNEY WITH CARE,
BUT SOMEHOW CHRISTMAS
DOESN'T SEEM QUITE THE SAME THIS YEAR"

ALL THE CHILDREN WERE TOSSING
ABOUT IN THEIR BEDS
WHILE VISIONS OF VAMPIRES
DANCED IN THEIR HEADS.

THE WIFE SHE WAS RESTLESS,
AND EVEN I BIT MY NAILS
IT SEEMED AS THOUGH FAR OFF
WE COULD HAER MANY WAILS.

THEN, FROM THE GRAVEYARD
THERE CAME SUCH A MOAN
IT MADE US ALL REALIZE
WE WERE NOT ALONE

I LOOKED THROUGH THE SHUTTERS
AND COULD SEE THROUGH THE CRACKS
A MINIATURE HEARSE
PULLED BY EIGHT LAUGHING BATS

THE DRIVER SHOUTED
AS ONWARD THEY CAME
HE LOVED THEM ALL DEARLY
AND CALLED THEM BY NAME

ON ZACHERLEY, ON GASPORT
ON LON CHANEY JR.
IF YOU'D ONLY PULL HARDER
WE'D GET THERE MUCH SOONER.

ON BELA, ON BORIS,
YOU TOO, FRANKENSTEIN,
ON WOLF MAN, ON MUMMY,
WE'RE WAY BEHIND TIME.

AND I SHUDDERED INSTINCTIVLY
AS I HEARD FROM THE SHINGLES
AN EAR PIERCING SCREAM
I KNEW WASN'T KRIS KRINGLES'

FROM UNDER THE FRONT WINDOW
CAME THE HOWL OF A DOG
SOMETHING CAME DOWN THE CHIMNEY
IT LOOKED LIKE A FOG.

AS THIS FOG TOOK SHAPE
IN FRONT OF THE FIRE
I KNEW THAT OLD SANTA
HAD BECOME A VAMPIRE.

HIS TEETH WERE SHARP FANGS
THERE WAS BLOOD IN HIS BEARD
AND JUST BEHIND HIM
TWO PALE LADIES APPEARED.

SAYING NARY A WORD
THEY WENT RIGHT TO WORK
PIERCING EVERYONES ARTERIES
WITHOUT EVEN A JERK

QUIETLY SIPPING
WITH AN INSATIABLE THIRST
THEY DRANK SO MUCH BLOOD
I THOUGHT THEY WOULD BURST

AND WHEN THEY WERE DONE
WITH A DRUNKEN LIKE GIGGLE
THEY SLID UNDER THE DOOR
WITH A CUTE LITTLE RIGGLE.

JUMPING INTO THE HEARSE
THEY FLEW OVER THE WALL
SHOUTING "FLAP AWAY! FLAP AWAY!
FLAP AWAY! ALL."

AND I HEARD HIM EXCLAIM
FROM THE DISTANCE AFAR
"MERRY CHRISTMAS TO ALL
WHATEVER YOU ARE!"

A monster-ized parody of "Twas the Night Before Christmas" was another viewer submission. Zach made it part of his December 25, 1959, show.

The New York Times

Times Square, New York 36   LA 4-1000

FIRST IN ADVERTISING IN THE WORLD'S FIRST MARKET

August 2, 1960

Mr. Zacherley, Director
Department of Tourism of Transylvania
c/o WOR-TV
1440 Broadway
New York, New York

Dear Mr. Zacherley:

Your program of last week which invited viewers to "visit
Transylvania" and "fly the vampire route" offers something delightfully different that should make a real killing in the
vacation field.

As you probably know, The New York Times is the world's
largest and best-read resort and travel guide. We can help
you bury your tourist problems.

New York Times readers are best-possible prospects for
vacations anytime and anywhere. So why not Transylvania? If
laid end to end our 1,350,000 readers would be stretched out
for 1,534 miles. That should please the most exacting Dracula.

The New York Times, you see, reaches leaders in every
group -- in business, industry, finance, the professions, go-
vernment and society. You can be sure that leading ghouls,
werewolves, warlocks, haunts, witches and poltergeists also
turn first to The Times when making vacation plans.

Bring in your Transylvania vacation advertisement before
the deadline. We'll be happy to show you our Morgue and other
principal points of interest.

Sincerely,

D.F. Beckham, Jr.
Travel Promotion Manager

D.F. Beckham, Jr.:ls

Seotember 26th, 1960

TO: Those Concerned   FROM: Mary Winters

Re: Zacherley — Fall Schedule (1960) in Los Angeles (KHJ—TV)

Playdate	Show #	Title
October 7th	1	MIGHT JOE YOUNG
October 14th	2	THE SAINT IN NEW YORK
October 21st	3	MURDER ON A HONEYMOON
October 28th	4	PASSPORT TO DESTINY
November 4th	5	ROAR OF THE DRAGON
November 11th	6	EMERGENCY CALL
November 18th	7	GENIUS AT WORK
November 25th	8	FORTY NAUGHTY GIRLS
December 2nd	9	THE BODY SNATCHERS
December 9th	10	MUMMY'S BOYS
December 16th	11	ZOMBIES ON BROADWAY
December 23rd	12	I WALKED WITH A ZOMBIE

TONIGHT AT HALF-PAST MIDNIGHT!

Direct from Transylvania

ZACHERLEY'S HORRORS

A frightening new series
for all living late night creatures,
Mummies, and Daddies who enjoy
movies in the blood tingling vein!

KHJ-TV / CHANNEL 9 / AN RKO GENERAL STATION

NICK KENNY
Zacherley Good For TV Kiddies

WE USED TO get mad at Zacherley when "Charnel" Nine's ghastly host for horror pictures used to inject himself into a fascinating show just at a crucial moment and ruin the suspense with his tomfoolery. Now we realize that the pasty-faced refugee from a movie mausoleum, in his own gruesome way, is really debunking terror-vision for a host of impressionable young fans. Instead of being terrorized by the pictures, they actually enjoy the pallid "monster" of ceremonies and they laugh at his antics. This is a step in the right direction.

N.Y. Daily Mirror —
May 3, 1960

Hot weather hilarity!
ZACHERLEY
Tonight at Midnight
Tomorrow at 1:30
PM on WOR-TV
channel 9

ABOVE AND FACING PAGE: Zach goes ghost-to-ghost! Our favorite horror host got some cross-country exposure when episodes of *Zacherley at 12* played on WOR's sister station in L.A., KHJ-TV. (See their schedule in the "Zacherley Potpourri" section.)

PASSPORT
DIPLOMATIC

The undersigned CREATURE is
hereby granted entrance th the
SOVERIEGN STATE OF TRANSYLVANIA
during the year 1960; the year
of the FRANKENSTEIN JUBILEE.

_____
last name first name alias

Creature CLASSIFICATION (*)

He-Wolf ___   Mummy   ___
She-Wolf ___   Ghoul   ___
Vampire ___   Monster ___
(c)check more THAN 3)
Special Markings: (Describe any
    prominent scars, lumps, etc.)

NMMOMMMMMSMSM_____

_____ CHECHRONIC
                 FANGOSIS
Innoculations:

Werewolf Fever ___ Fur Fallout ___
Moon Sickness ___ Egyptian
Coffinitis   ___   Itch ___
Mummyosis   ___ Scaley Skin ___
Sunrayphobia   ___ Vampyra
Banana Blight ___ Mania ___
                   GREE FEVER
                   GHOULING

Authority
AUTHORITY
AUTHORITY
This PASSPORT is issued by
the AMMBASSADOR-AT-LARGE with
the understanding and condition
that the BEARER CREATURE will
travel only during the hours
of DARKNESS and will do no EXCA-
VATING in the State GRAVEYARDS
after visiting hours.
Wolf-calling is restricted
to nights of the FULL MOON.

SPACE
FOR
CREATURE
PICTURE

AMBASSADOR-
AT-LARGE

ABOVE AND FACING PAGE: *Cocoa Marsh chocolate syrup was a sponsor of Zacherley at 12. One of their promotions was a Transylvania passport designed by Zach.*

GREEN AND GOLD

He's Real Ghoul, Man

By Bruce Wieworka

After watching Zacherly for the last few years and becoming a fan of his from afar, the curiosity about this renowned television star gripped my friend Ralph and myself to the point where we thought it would be exciting and interesting to meet "The Master Ghoul." We managed to dig up the address of the studio from which Zach's show was taped and then assembled a dummy for him to massacre on his program. Shortly after receiving and using the dummy, His Excellancy from Transylvania sent us a letter of thanks and invited us to meet him personally one night while the show was being taped. We met at the appointed spot and waited, expecting him to appear amid fire and brimstone and accompanied by a cheerful group of werewolves, bats and black cats. Imagine our surprise when a tall, good-looking gentleman approached us and asked, "Are you Bruce and Ralph, the boys who sent me the dummy?" Surprised that he was wearing a light grey suit instead of a shroud, I managed to utter "yes" nervously but his easy going smile soon put us at ease and we began talking as if we had dug up graves together for years, and when he told us that he'd show us how his program was run, we were as happy as vampires in a bloodbank.

After showing us around and introducing us to the crew of cameramen, technicians and the director, he asked us if we'd like to help him work his show. Naturally, we jumped at the chance. We held props, helped him with his costumes and also made up signs for him to use. We had the run of the place and scurried about like werewolves in a crowded morgue. We ran out for spider sandwiches and coffee for the crew and in general became pretty handy to have around. Every week Ralph and I would meet Zacherley and run through the show. Then after the show we would stop for a bite (we'd bite anyone) and pretty soon we got to know each other pretty well. In my wildest dreams, I never imagined that Zacherley, the landlord of the house of horror, and I would be on terms that Frankenstein and the Wolfman would envy.

Let me set you straight on a couple of things. Contrary to popular belief, Zacherley's favorite dring is not Bloody Marys (with real blood). It's Cocoa Marsh and Yum Berry, on and off the T.V. screen. Also while being looked upon as a menace to civilization by some people, he's actually as generous and gentle as a big kid, and has to be refrained from giving people the gravel from Isobel's coffin. He even tries to pawn Gasport off on friends of short acquaintance.

In closing, I wish to say that now that I have known Zach for nearly three months, I am proud to say, he is a wonderful person as well as a brilliant performer; one of the few people in a high pressure world that can honestly be called "regular." There is no evidence of swell-headedness at all in his makeup and while I was thrilled to meet Zacherley the performer, I am proud to say I now know Zacherley, the human being. It's a great pleasure!

TRANSYLVANIA COLLEGE, Lexington 7, Kentucky
Office of Admissions

August 10, 1960

Department of Public Relations
WOR-TV
New York, New York

Gentlemen:

The year 1780 saw the founding of Transylvania University, since changed to Transylvania College, the first institution of higher learning west of the Allegheny Mountains. Throughout the years, the school has been dedicated to the preparation of young people for positions of leadership and responsible. Among others, our former students include two Vice Presidents of the United States; the President of the Confederate States of America; more than fifty United States Senators; five speakers of the House of Representatives; more than one hundred members of the House of Representatives; thirty-four ambassadors; and many others who have contributed much to the development of this country.

We are now told that the mention of Transylvania in the New York area often invokes laughs, chuckles, and chortles as the result of the antics of a television personality known as Zacherly.

Gentlemen, I wonder if you agree with us that this is an injustice to one of the country's finest small, liberal arts colleges?

We know not what alternative to suggest, but we hope that Zacherly can adopt another alma mater, the mention of which will be less offensive to our many friends, alumni, and prospective students in the greater New York area.

We look forward to hearing of any assistance you can give concerning this problem.

Sincerely yours,

Fred A. Lawson
Assistant Director of Admissions

Another moaner heard from! (The original was too light for reproduction; this is a re-typing.)

JOHN ZACHERLE   FROM: WOR TV PRESS DEPT.
                                              July 8, 1960

              BIOGRAPHICAL ANECDOTES

Marital status: Still single!

Age: 42 and ageing every day

Birthplace: Philadelphia, Pa.

Education: University of Pennsylvania, B.A. 1940

Service: Army, World War II. Captain (way behind the lines) (mostly)

Career: Actor, Philadelphia area
                  quarter season summer stock; hated it. (too much brainwork
                              learning lines)
                  Actor "Action in the Afternoon" one year CBS Network half-hour
                              daily show. Originated from WCAU, 1955,
                              in Philadelphia. Character parts.
                  Nighttime spook part assigned on basis of kookie undertaker
                              during one of the weekly "Action" series.
                  Played character known as "Ro-land" as host to shock movies
                              on WCAU for one year.
                  Played "Zacherley" on ABC TV New York, 1958

                  CURRENTLY: "Zacherley" show over WOR TV, New York, since
                              fall of 1959

Guest spots: 6 appearances on "Pat Boone Show", 1959
                              "Pat Boone" one of most ardent Zack
                              fans on earth.
                  "Dave Garroway's Today" show, 6/1/60. (Mr. Garroway is
                              apparently as insane about Zack as
                              Boone ever dreamed of; does imitations
                              around the house to keep the family
                              in line!)
                  Even appeared on the "Jack Paar Show" in December, 1958.
                              (Paar not available for comment after
                              the show. Charlie Weaver an obvious
                              Transylvanian.)

Residence: Commute weekends to Flourtown, Pa., where lives my dear
                              little old grey-haired mother.

Family: Have two older brothers and one sister...all married...all
                              enjoying the fun of this TV notoriety.

Pets: No pets around the house. Would like a nice friendly werewolf.

Desires: Would love to make a movie spoofing the whole "horror" theme
                              along the lines of "Zacherley" TV
                              presentation. (Anyone got some money?)

                  Like to play golf but never do.

                  Hope to take a vacation....

                  Want to get back to Italy someday.

                  Enjoy fixing things around the house...anybody's house.

After the end of Zach's one season at WOR, he typed out this "résumé."

Cape Cod Standard Times 8-2-60

At the Summer Theaters

Acting in Dennis Production Proves Highly Entertaining

DENNIS, Aug. 2—Those who like their comedy with a strong dash of the macabre will find that Playwright Charles Robinson has done the most to build up a sophisticated thriller around the lives of a couple of college professors and their wives. The production which opened last night at the Cape Playhouse does him justice.

It is not so much the mystery—there is really none—as the first act reveals and executes the contemplated murder, as the display of flamboyant affrontery of Mephistophilian professor on his sabbatical which evokes and creates the hilarious situation and quips of "Memo for a Green Thumb."

Edward Mulhare radiates refined rascality. Louise Latham gives a good portrayal of the spouse whose horticultural passion leads to an untimely grave. Kramer the postman, whose yen for gardening is the key to the solution of the macabre happenings at the Rodman home, was amusingly personified by Archie Smith.

Looking breathtakingly lovely and blending sophistication with naivity with great charm was Nan Martin in the role of the colleague's wife. Mimi Bondra as the campus "sloosy" and John Zacherle as the serious colleague gave creditable performances.

The most subtle acting last night was rendered by Doug Lambert as Cushing, the undergraduate whose dubious, but nonetheless urgent quest for the professor's taped lectures, adds to the suspense, in this at times hairraising comedy.

Scenery and lighting were expertly employed and were especially effective in conveying the atmosphere of eeriness that pervades the latter part of the play.

Shouts of "Bravo" acclaimed the cast for numerous curtain calls.

E. M. D.

Cape Playhouse ★

DENNIS ON CAPE COD
MASSACHUSETTS

America's most famous Summer Theatre

On Route 6A
CHARLES MOONEY, MANAGING DIRECTOR
34th SEASON
PHONE DENNIS 60 or 175
Evenings at 8:30 — Matinees Wednesday and Thursday at 2:30 p.m.
Prices—Evenings: $3.95 to $1.50 Matinees: $3.50 to $1.00
Box Office open from 10:00 a.m. to 9:30 p.m. daily except Sunday
Ticket reservations will be held until 5 p.m. Evenings and 1 p.m. Matinees

MONDAY, AUGUST 1 THRU SATURDAY, AUGUST 6
THE CAPE PLAYHOUSE
of Raymond Moore Foundation

presents

EDWARD MULHARE

in

MEMO FOR A GREEN THUMB

A New Comedy-Mystery
by CHARLES ROBINSON

with

NAN MARTIN

LOUISE LATHAM   ARCHIE SMITH
DOUG LAMBERT   MIMI VONDRA

and

JOHN ZACHERLE

Directed by KURT KASZNAR

Sets by HELEN POND   Lighting by THOMAS GARRETT

THE GAY NINETIES

Relax and Enjoy Good Food and Drink
DELICIOUS MEALS -- ALL BEVERAGES
Ye Olden Tavern Atmosphere
Visit the GIFT SHOPPE
Route 28, West Yarmouth

Regarding the play Memo for a Green Thumb, *Zach recalls: "One day during its run, I was out on the beach on Cape Cod and laid down. The day before was a wet day and the beach was still chilly, and the chill of that sand kicked off an attack of kidney stones! It was very painful. I went into the hospital — I don't know how they [the* Green Thumb *company] covered for my part."*

Cool Ghoul Back –In Stage Show

JOHN ZACHERLE

. . . as Roland

REMEMBER Roland, the TV friend of werewolves, vampires and all manner of ghoulish creatures who were a part of his Channel 10 late night show some seasons ago?

In his Dracula-like make-up, he attracted a large fan following here as he filled in station breaks and introduced commercials during the late movies.

Roland is coming back to town—but not in horror makeup. Under his right name, John Zacherle, he has won an important featured role as Odysseus, King of Ithaca, in the new Broadway musical, "La Belle." The show is based on Offenbach's "La Belle Helene," the story of Helen of Troy. It opens in Philadelphia at the Shubert, Aug. 14. Zacherle will sing, dance and do a bit of clowning in his first Broadway musical comedy role.

—TV-RADIO—

Child-star Thomas with Zacherley: Radar begins in a bat's ears

NBC

▶1, 2, 3—Go! Sundays on NBC, has hopes of successfully combining travel, education, and entertainment. Produced by Jack Kuney, a producer-director of the syndicated "Play of the Week" and a red-hot papa who has declared war on "crud like Roy Rogers," his new one will be a weekly potpourri centered around a single theme. On the Halloween show, for example, Kuney will send his 10-year-old hero, Richard Thomas, and the ghoul-specialist Zacherley off to a haunted house, where Richard will learn that bats have radar-like ears, that witches don't even have broomsticks, and that there are a number of more imposing bogies in the world, like hunger and poverty, which he can help thwart by giving his trick-or-treat collections to UNICEF.

Thayer David, Mimi Turque, Menasha Skulnik, Joan Diener, Howard Da Silva, John Zacherle and Lette Rehnolds in a scene for "La Belle," which centers on Helen of Troy. Mr. Skulnik, who appeared in many song and dance shows on the Yiddish stage, will be appearing in his first Broadway musical. He will portray the leading role of Menelaus.

CASH BOX – JAN. 14, 1961

Odd Double Bill

—A recent edition of WAEB disk jockey Kerm Gregory's
, Castle Rock, saw more than 2,000 teenagers turn out to
nd Zacherley. Vee performed his latest Library hit, "Rub-
rley did some of the bits which he does on his Elektra LP,
Zacherley."

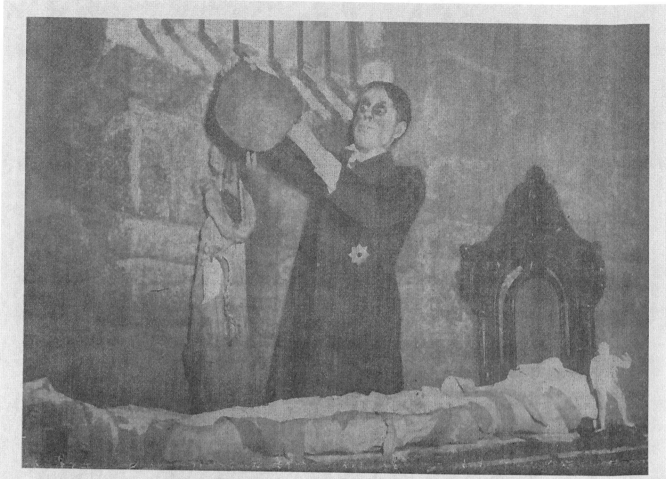

(NEWS foto by Frank Hurley)

Creepy Time Down South

South Transylvania, that is, where everybody's ogre, Zacherley, is monster of ceremonies at 7:30 P.M. Saturdays on WPIX-TV's Chiller Theatre, headquarters for horror hobbyists. Zach holds Phyllis, amorous amoeba whose search for boy friend is complicated by fact that she keeps dividing. Mummy sacked out on table is Charley, who dropped in for year's nap between scare movies.

Come the fall of 1963 and Zach was back — two more clicks up the dial, on New York's WPIX Channel 11. He hosted Chiller Theatre *(showing mostly "newer" titles like* Attack of the 50 Foot Woman *and* Plan 9 from Outer Space*) and also appeared on weekday afternoons, showing Hercules cartoons and Three Stooges shorts!*

1963 WPIX·TV N.Y.

LIVING IN A
LAUNDRY HAMPER!

(FOR THE ENTIRE SEASON --
-TOO CHEAP TO GET A
WOODEN CRATE MADE!)

(AND THEY ALSO HAD BAD MOVIES
TO SHOW!)   (Z)

ABOVE: *Zach in his wife's "coffin" (actually a laundry hamper!) at WPIX.* BELOW: *Read the comment he wrote on the back of this photo!*

5

DISC·O·TEEN

ZACH WAS DROPPED BY WPIX IN MAY 1964, AS WAS FLOOR DIRECTOR BARRY LANDERS. BARRY SUBSEQUENTLY MET WITH FRED SAYLES, PROGRAM DIRECTOR FOR A NEW MULTI-LANGUAGE UHF STATION IN NEWARK, NEW JERSEY, AND PITCHED AN IDEA: AN ENGLISH-LANGUAGE *AMERICAN BANDSTAND*-STYLE MUSIC AND DANCE SHOW CALLED *DISC-O-TEEN*. WHEN BARRY MENTIONED HE HAD WORKED WITH JOHN ZACHERLE, SAYLES ASKED, "DO YOU THINK WE COULD GET HIM?" BARRY HAD A MEETING WITH ZACHERLE, WHO AGREED TO HOST IN HIS ZACHERLEY MAKEUP AND COSTUME. THE SHOW FEATURED MUSIC GROUPS MADE UP OF LOCAL HIGH SCHOOLERS COMPETING FOR THE CHANCE TO WIN A RECORDING CONTRACT.

Going to rock concerts was a lot cheaper in those days!

ABOVE: *From time to time, well-known rock bands appeared on* Disc-O-Teen. *Here's Zach with the Greenwich Village group The Blues Project.* BELOW: *Zach and the Box Tops on the 1967 Halloween episode.* Disc-O-Teen *premiered in May 1965 and ran for two and a half years.*

MONSTER MASH—The cool ghoul of Channel 47's Disc-O-Teen, Zacherly, shows the Lovin' Spoonfuls, rock 'n' roll group, how to liven up the monster mash with some new go-go steps.

On the Cover

Cool Ghoul Enchants Teen Fans

By RUTH ANN BURNS

Knock, knock. Squeeeeek—eek—thud. "Yes?" a deep, measured voice asks questioningly. "Can I have tickets for the Wednesday Disc-o-Teen," a tiny voice asks, its owner waiting breathlessly for a reply.

"Why of course, of course," booms Zacherly, lovable monster and ghostly host of Channel 47's live "Disc-o-Teen," that broadcasts six times a week at 6 p.m. from the station's Newark studios.

No sooner was the squeaky door unbolted than about 20 taeen-age girls piled into the cluttered den seeking autographs, pictures of singing groups, and just a chance to be with their favorite master of ceremonies.

Wildly Unpredictable

Zacherly, whose real name is John Zacherle, has the only live teen dance show in the Greater New York area and the largest broadcasting studio. Barry Landers, co-producer with Zacherly, describes his star as a "you-your type person, rather than an I-me personality that many well known people become. John is a perfect talent with a unique and wild sense of humor that is so unpredictable that I never count on a script being followed all the way," said the South Plainfield resident, who

produced Zacherly's show on Channel 11 and also the Clay Cole show.

Dressed in very ordinary clothes before the show, Zacherly is not at all recognizable as the cool ghoul who delights both adults and youngsters with his macabre sense of humor. The TV veteran of monster shows, who traveled from channel 6 to 9 to 7 to 11 to 47, admitted the startling fact that he was never allowed to watch monster programs or movies as a child.

Crash Study Course

"When I was first assigned to play a monster I saw about 50 horrible movies and decided that monsters were actually funny in a way, so I got the idea to be a comic ghoul," said the versatile actor.

"It all started when I played an undertaker in an old cowboy movie and wore the black coat and tails; it reminded me of a monster," said Zacherly thoughtfully.

Last February, Channel 47 decided to launch a teen dance show and thought Zacherly would be an unusual host but one with magnetic qualities for attracting teen-agers to the program. "I write all my material and the idea is a show that is fun and offffers opportunities for amateur dance bands to appear on television," said the openly warm star.

(Continued on Page 22)

Cool Ghoul

(Continued from Page 3)

"Disc-o-Teen" is unique in every way. "This is the only show (on TV) where amateur bands can play. We have one on each day and have debuted more than 200 bands on live TV," Zacherly said.

The show now is staging a contest in which a band can win a recording session. According to Landers, over 5,000 requests from bands throughout New Jersey have come in so far.

While amateur bands provide the live entertainment on weekdays, the Saturday slot is reserved for well known names such as Sonny and Cher, the Dave Clark Five, the Lovin' Spoonfuls, Rolling Stones and Tom Jones.

The band playing on a daily telecast brings 50 couples from its high school to dance on the show.

Looking fondly at the bouncing, vibrant, high school students, Zacherly said, "We let them wear what they want and there is no restriction that a girl must have a boy to dance with. In the beginning it was hard getting students to come because no one knew about it, and girls dance more so there always are more females than males."

A glance around the dance floor backed up his statement, with teen-agers dancing with complete abandonment and arrayed in the latest "mod" fashions from London. There were bell-bottomed slacks galore, dungarees, and even op dresses.

The girls get a chance to "go-go" on a box with the camera zeroing in for a close-up, and generally they didn't mind dancing alone or with another girl.

Quick-Change

Zacherly can get dressed for the show in 3½ minutes flat, including makeup. "I'm afraid these rags will disintegrate some day as I rush into them," said the friendly MC, starting sadly at his well known trademark.

Whomp, went an inked stamper on Zach's head, leaving clearly emblazoned: ''Teen Disc-o-Tek, admit 2." "Can you see it?" asked the talented star, already improvising for the day's show.

Volunteer helpers swarm in and out of the office addressing postcards and opening over 200 letters a day that fans send. "Rather like on-the-job training for the postal card association, don't you think?" asked Zacherly.

"A live show is much more dynamic than a videotaped one, and I got tired of lip-moving ventriloquists who don't sing. Why, pretty soon it will be a lip reading world with soundless conversations," commented Zach, going through all the motions of speech but with no noise coming out.

The wildest skits are done with a hairy ape dubbed Barry McGuire by Zacherly. It is introduced as a man who reverted to an ape after worrying so much about the end of the world. Teaching the ape to speak and eat again involves the help of the teen-agers who usually get slurpy whipped cream kisses in return.

The reaction of the teens to his wild sense of humor is enthusiastic. "Will you marry me, Zacherly?" "Would you go to my senior prom next Saturday?" These are some of the requests the lovable actor gets from his female fans.

So Handsome!

One exhuberant young girl said, "You feel like he really cares about you, he has a fabulous personality, and besides he is just gorgeous without his makeup!"

"I enjoy meeting all the teens now who used to watch my old shows and say how scared they would be, glued to their TV sets," said the show's star. "Many of them send me these charming little monsters of Nibbishes and original monster paintings that decorate my den," he said laughing.

Still talking to his fans after the show, Zacherlp helped clean the set, then jumped on his Zach-mobile, taking off for Transylvania until the next show.

New Jersey Television Broadcasting Corp.

MEMORANDUM

MARCH 13, 1967

TO: PETER BRYSAC, JACK WILSON, ALLEN GOMEZ

FROM: ED COOPERSTEIN

I ASK YOU TO KEEP THE FOLLOWING IN CONFIDENCE REGARDING CERTAIN
COMPLAINTS I HAVE GOTTEN INVOLVING SUGGESTIVE CAMERA WORK ON THE
DISC-O-TEEN SHOWS.

SINCE I HAVE DONE A LOT OF DIRECTING MYSELF, I KNOW HOW IMPORTANT
IT IS - PARTICULARLY ON SUCH AN AD-LIB SHOW - TO GIVE CAMERAMEN
FREEDOM ON SUCH A SHOW. WHAT I THINK YOU AS DIRECTORS HAVE TO BE
VERY CAREFUL ABOUT ARE THE MANY SUGGESTIVE SHOTS WHICH OCCUR IN THE
CAMERMAN'S "OVER-ENTHUSIASM", PARTICULARLY WITH PRETTY LITTLE GIRLS
HOPPING AROUND.

I DON'T THINK I NEED ELABORATE TO YOU WHAT I MEAN, BUT LET'S BE
ESPECIALLY CAREFUL - WITHOUT BEING PRUDISH - ABOUT BUST SHOTS, FANNY
SHOTS, ETC. I LEAVE IT TO YOUR OWN GOOD TASTE AND JUDGEMENT HOW TO
HANDLE THIS ON A DAILY BASIS.

EUGENE M. GRAY

18 EAST 9TH ROAD

BROAD CHANNEL N.Y. (11693)

SEPTEMBER 20, 1967.

DISC- O- TEEN

ZACHERLEY

WNJU T. V.

1020 BROAD STREET

NEWARK N.J. (07102)

DEAR MR. ZACHERLEY,

I REPRESENT A VOCAL GROUP KNOWN AS, " LISA DANNIELS
AND THE DYNIMICS". THEY HAVE PLAYED MANY CLUBS IN THE ROCKAWAY
AND QUEENS AREA, AND THEY ALSO HAVE A VERY LARGE FOLLOWING.

WE WATCH YOUR T. V. SHOWS, AND MANY TIMES HAVE SEEN
GROUPS GET GOOD EXPOSURE. WE WOULD BE GREATFUL IF YOU WOULD
CONSIDER HELPING US. THERE ARE TAPES AVAILABLE THAT WE CAN SEND,
OR WE CAN COME IN PERSON, WHICH EVER IS CONVENIENT.

IF YOU CAN HELP US, OR GIVE US SOME GOOD ADVISE ON
HOW WE CAN GET MORE EXPOSURE, WE WOULD BE MOST GREATFUL. YOUR
EARLIEST ACKNOWLEDGEMENT OF THIS MATTER WILL BE GREATLY APPRECIATED.

SINCERELY YOURS,

EUGENE M. GRAY   MGR.

NEWARK STAR LEDGER ~ 2/17/91

Rock'n'ghoul reunion really hops

'Disc-O Teen' dancers break out the old go-go boots and camp it up with horror host Zacherle

— By JAY LUSTIG —

"Disc-O-Teen," a television dance show taped from 1965 to 1967 at a studio in Newark's Mosque Theater (now Symphony Hall) was great, said Joette Martin of Nutley, one of the show's regular dancers, "because you'd be able to dance an hour a day for nothing. It was a continuous party."

That party continued for one more night, as approximately 80 dancers and crew members, as well as the show's beloved host, John Zacherle, gathered at the Hop nightclub in Totowa earlier this month for a one-of-a-kind reunion.

Fittingly, the "Disc-O-Teen" graduates enthusiastically crowded the club's dance floor, but more importantly they had a chance to renew friendships and refresh memories. Footage from the old shows, which were aired five and sometimes six days a week on UHF Channel 47, was shown, and old snapshots were displayed.

Known to most of the Disc-O-Teeners as "Zach," Zacherle changed into one of his customary ghoul costumes soon after the reunion began, and played the part of Sonny in a lip-synched version of Sonny & Cher's "I Got You Babe," as he did in one of the most memorable "Disc-O-Teen" skits.

Zacherle, who was a radio disc jockey for many years after the show ended and has recently worked as the host of a series of horror videos, stayed in touch with the dancers for a while after the show was canceled. "But then I went downhill with my Christmas cards," he said. "A few of them I heard from, but the majority I really lost track of."

He said the reunion was exciting, because "these were all high school kids, and now they're somewhere around 40 years old, a lot of them with families and all, and they just look great. It's like finding a lost family.

"I wasn't aware at the time of how much that show meant to the kids, especially the Jersey kids. Mostly girls would show up, of course, and a few reluctant boys. We started inviting schools to come in, too. We had busloads of kids come in from schools all over the place, and they would often bring their own high school rock bands, and they would get up and play 'The House of the Rising Sun' or something like that."

"Disc-O-Teen" was taped Monday through Friday (with extra shows sometimes taped during the week and aired on Saturdays) in the late afternoon. Dancers had just enough time after school, said Martin, "to run to the bus, go home and change into something a lot

Please turn to Page 4

'Disc-O-Teen' star John Zacherle reminisces at the Hop in Totowa . . . 'It's like finding a lost family'

'60s hoofers hop to rock'n'ghoul reunion

Continued from Page One

hipper, like your white go-go boots."

"If they liked the way you danced, you would be invited back," said Nancy Semon of Toms River, "and they counted on you because you held a position on the dance floor. But anybody could get on the show."

In addition to providing a place for local bands to get exposure, "Disc-O-Teen" booked major rock acts of the day, who would lip-synch their hit songs as the teenagers danced. The Doors appeared on "Disc-O-Teen," as did the Lovin' Spoonful, the Rascals and many bands—such as the Blues Magoos, the Critters, the Box Tops, the Left Banke and Every Mother's Son—now forgotten to all but the most ardent fans of '60s rock.

The lip-synching was done out of necessity. "We weren't set up to rehearse anything," said Zacherle, "because they had back-to-back shows in this big room. It was a great big studio, and the minute one show was over, on the other side of the studio—there were no walls or anything like that—another show would start up.

"In fact, someone was always on before we were, so we never had a chance to get a band up there and practice. The engineers didn't have the time

to get a balance and all that kind of thing. It was one of the things that was tough for the high school bands, too, because they did play live."

Comedy skits, centered around Zacherle's campy horror act, completed the content of a typical show. "He used to do little vampire skits in between the rock music," said Semon. "It was pretty bizarre: It was like a Fellini movie, because you'd have these normal kids dancing, and you'd have a guy who is a vampire chopping up his wife, who was made of Jell-O.

"My mother used to worry about us when we went on the show."

The "Disc-O-Teen" dancers got a further taste of show business when Zacherle brought them to concerts he hosted in New York's Central Park. The dancers also appeared as the opening act of a Mosque Theater concert by the Rolling Stones.

Later, when they entered the working world, an unusually high number of the dancers chose creative fields. No one believes this to be coincidental.

"Being on a TV show that young, and dancing, and meeting all different types of people, and then going to the concerts and meeting people, you just don't think of a 9-to-5 existence," said Semon, who has worked as a writer, editor and publicist, and handled publicity for the reunion. "We were exposed

to a lot more than most kids our age, and a lot of us went on to do weird things."

"We were neighborhood kids, mostly from Newark, and it opened up a whole realm of possibilities," said Martin, a commercial artist who organized the reunion with Christine Domaniecki of Belleville, an actress. "We met photographers there, and professional musicians, and public relations people.

"I sent out questionnaires to everyone, asking 'What are you doing now?' About half of them are teachers, but a lot of people went into TV production or art of some kind. There are a few music producers who came out of groups that were on the show. That type of thing attracts creative people, even when they are kids. It was the hippest kids who went down there, unless they went with a school trip."

Martin identified one more way in which the show was a positive influence on the teenagers who appeared on it.

"Zach being such a wonderful guy, as he still is, made all the difference for a lot of us," she said. "He rescued so many stranded kids, and doled out bus fare to other kids who got down there and couldn't get home. He drove kids home who were in trouble, and talked to parents and smoothed stuff down. He was just a wonder through the whole thing."

6

A ZACHERLEY POTPOURRI

CONTRACTS, SCRIPTS, AND MORE!

ON THE FOLLOWING PAGES IS THE SCRIPT FOR ROLAND'S PRESENTATION OF *DRACULA'S DAUGHTER* **(1936). IT MAY BE THE ONLY SURVIVING ROLAND SCRIPT.**

SHOCK THEATRE
SAT. MAY 10, 1958
DRACULAS DAUGHTER

ET THEME, BG FOR

SLIDE 450   BOOTH ANNCR: SHOCK THEATER!

SLIDE MDM   TONIGHT, DRACULAS DAUGHTER

SLIDE 427   WITH YOUR HOST, ROLAND

ROLAND PREPARING LOST & FOUND   I AM ROLAND AND I'VE LOST AN AMOEBA. I KNEW
NOTICE

THELMA COULDN'T BE TRUSTED, BUT YOU KNOW HE HAD A

WAY WITH HIMSELF! HE SAID HE WANTED TO SLIDE

AROUND ON THE JAGGED ROCKS UP ABOVE, AND NO

SOONER DID I TAKE HIS LEASH OFF THAN HE WAS GONE.

SO I'M PUTTING OUT AN ALL POINTS BULLETIN FOR

THELMA THE BOY AMOEBA. YOU MIGHT WANT TO TAKE

DOWN HIS DESCRIPTION, SO YOU DON'T MISTAKE HIM FOR

SOME OTHER AMOEBA --

NAME -- THELMA. HEIGHT, 5 $\frac{1}{2}$ INCHES. LENGTH,

3 FEET. WIDTH, 1 ft. 3 inches. WEIGHT, 36 POUNDS.

COMPLEXION, BAD. VERY BAD. EYES: COLORLESS.

OUTSTANDING CHARACTERISTICS: THIS AMOEBA IS

TRANSPARANT, CAN FLY, HAS NO KNOWN MEANS OF

SUPPORT BUT SPRITZES. HIS BIG WEAKNESS IS LEFT

HEART VENTRICLES. IF YOU SEE THELMA, LOTS

OF LUCK.

TONIGHT, I SHALL TELL YOU THE STORY OF TRANSYLVANIAS

FIRST LADY DEBUTANTE, DRACULA'S DAUGHTER!

PGM FILM 10:30

BREAK #1   SET

AUDIO OUTCUE: WOLFCALL

OF COURSE HE WAS GONE! WHAT DID THEY EXPECT A

SPIRITED YOUNG GIRL LIKE THAT TO DO? LEAVE

HER DADDY IN THAT DRAB PINE BOX?

(MY DEAR)

AH MY DEAR, YOU'RE AWAKE AGAIN. (TO CAMERA)

I HOPE SHE DIDN'T CATCH ON TO THAT BUSINESS

WITH THELMA. SHE'S REALLY BEEN BOTHERING ME FOR

A PET OF SOME KIND.

AH, MY DEAR, YOU'RE LOOKING SPLENDID, BUT, WELL,

YOUR HAIR, REALLY, I THINK I'D BETTER DO SOMETHING

WITH IT.

I'D SEND FOR THAT HAIR FIXING COUSIN OF YOURS

IF I KNEW WHERE TO FIND HIM...

VASELINE HAIR TONIC
SPIC AND SPAN

MY DEAR, I THINK YOU'RE GOING TO NEED A COMPLETE

OVERHAULING SOON. YOU'RE GETTING TOO RESTLESS.

(HITS STAKE)

CONFOUND THAT THELMA! IF HE WOULD HAVE BEHAVED

HIMSELF I COULD HAVE TRAINED HIM AND PRESENTED

MY DEAR WITH A FINE PET. IF YOU SHOULD BE ON

THE LOOKOUT FOR THELMA, REMEMBER THAT HE'S MAD

FOR LEFT HEART VENTRICLES! AND HE LIKES TO

CRAWL IN THE WOODS AT NIGHT!

PGM FILM 10:30

116

BREAK #2   SAT

AUDIO OUTCUE :   IF THERE'S A WAY TO CLEAR YOU,
I'LL DO IT!

THAT VON HELSING JUST NEVER GIVES UP. THE ONLY
THING HE EVER SAID THAT WAS RIGHT WAS WHEN HE
TRIED TO TELL EVERYONE COUNT DRACULA WAS A
VAMPIRE. OF COURSE HE WAS A VAMPIRE, AND ONE OF
THE BEST IN THE BUSINESS! AND HE DIDN'T JUST
RUN AFTER PRETTY GIRLS. HE'D PUT THE BITE ON
ANYBODY WHO REALLY NEEDED HELP!

YOU PROBABLY THINK COUNT DRACULA'S DAUGHTER WAS
A BIT OF AN INGRATE, BURNING UP HER DADDY LIKE
SHE DID, BUT SHE WAS A REAL MIXED UP GIRL. THE
FIRE DIDN'T HURT THE OLD BOY ONE BIT, ALTHO IGOR
AND I DID GET A FEW NASTY BURNS DRAGGING THE
COUNT AWAY FROM THE FIRE. THAT'S WHY I WAS
UNABLE TO ATTEND THE COCKTAIL PARTY THAT WAS
HELD IN MY HONOR.

DRISTAN
PALMOLIVE

PGM FILM 14:05

BREAK #3   SAT.

AUDIO OUTCUE: PLEASE DON'T COME ANY CLOSER!

(SCREAM)

ROLAND WITH MASK IN FRONT
OF FACE, REMOVES SAME

NOW WHAT DO YOU SUPPOSE LILLY WAS AFRAID OF? THE

COUNTESS WAS A FINE ARTIST. AS   A MATTER OF

FACT, SHE PAINTED IGOR. NOT HIS PICTURE -- SHE JUST

PAINTED HIM ALL OVER -- AND HE LOOKED REMARKABLY

IMPROVED. NATURALLY, THE FIRST THING HE DID

WAS TO RUN DOWN TO HIS BROTHERS TAVERN SO HE

COULD SHOW OFF IN FRONT OF HIS FRIENDS!

NEWPORT
SUNOCO

AS YOU CAN IMAGINE, I WAS DELIGHTED TO KNOW THAT

COUNT DRACULA'S DAUGHTER WAS NOT WASTING HER

GIFTED TALENT.

THE ONLY THING THAT BOTHERED ME WAS THE FACT THAT

SHE DIDN'T TAKE HER VICTIMS ALL THE WAY ACROSS THE

LINE IF YOU KNOW WHAT I MEAN. SHE KEPT THE

AMBULANCES RUNNING DAY AND NIGHT!

PGM FILM 12:10

BREAK #4   SAT.

AUDIO OUTCUE: SAND - TAKE HER TO THE CAR.

IF I WOULD HAVE BEEN SANDA, I WOULD HAVE TAKEN
THAT MEDDLING LITTLE FOOL TO DR. YOGAMI. HE
WOULD HAVE TURNED HER INTO A WEREWOLF AND
SHIPPED HER BACK TO TIBET. YOU OUGHT TO SEE
HIS PLACE, WAY UP THERE IN THE FORBIDDEN MOUNTAINS.
I'LL BET HE'S GOT OVER 800 DANCING WEREWOLFS IN
HIS HERD. HE'S QUITE A TRAINER HIMSELF -- HE'S
ALWAYS PLAYING GUESSING GAMES WITH HIS WEREWOLVES :

M&M
BROMO SELTZER

YOU KNOW THAT BUSINESS WITH LILLY, THE YOUNG
LADY WHO WANTED HER PICTURE PAINTED? I'VE ALWAYS
SUSPECTED SHE KNEW THE COUNTESS WAS A VAMPIRE,
BECAUSE SHE WAS ALWAYS TELLING HER FRIENDS SHE
WOULD JUST LOVE TO FREE LOAD IN THE LOCAL
HOSPITAL FOR A COUPLE OF WEEKS :

PGM FILM 10:25

BREAK #5   SAT.

VIDEO OUTCUE:

BROADCAST MONTAGE

NOW CAN YOU BLAME THE PEOPLE FOR COMPLAINING ABOUT

HIGH TAXES? ALL THAT TROUBLE AND EXPENSE

TO FIND A WORTHLESS SECRETARY WHO WAS LUCKY

ENOUGH TO MEET A GENUINE VAMPIRE! AND ON TOP OF IT,

AN ALL EXPENSE PAID TRIP TO TRANSYLVANIA! IF IT

HAD HAPPENED TO ANYONE WITH AN OUNCE OF SENSE

YOU KNOW WHAT THEY'D SAY...

FAB
COL. DENT. CREAM

AS THEY SAY IN TRANSYLVANIA, LIKE FATHER, LIKE

DAUGHTER! AND, ALL BATS COME HOME TO REST IN

TRANSYLVANIA. THE COUNTESS WAS ON HER WAY, AND

BEETLE BRAIN VON HELSING WAS RIGHT ON THE JOB!

PGM FILM 10:30

CLOSE   SAT.

A HUNDRED YEARS AGO MY FOOT. IT WAS 200 YEARS
AGO AND I WAS THERE. IT WAS ONE OF THOSE SILLY
ACCIDENTS. ONE NIGHT WE ALL TURNED INTO BATS
AND WERE PRACTICING POWER DIVES, AND SHE NEVER
PULLED OUT IN TIME! THAT'S PART OF THE FUN OF
BEING A VAMPIRE. SOMETIME I'LL TELL YOU ABOUT
THE THIRD TIME I DIED, THAT WAS THE BEST!
(IGOR)
OF COURSE I'D LIKE A SPIDER HOAGY -- WHY DON'T YOU
RUN DOWN TO YOUR UNCLE'S PLACE AND GET A DOZEN!

OXYDOL

NEXT WEEK I'M GOING TO TELL YOU ABOUT DR. RENAULT'S
SECRET AND CRY OF THE WEREWOLF.

GOODNIGHT -- WHATEVER YOU ARE!

ZACH'S JOURNAL

DURING THE TUMULTUOUS TIME WHEN JOHN ZACHERLE WAS TRYING TO MOVE FROM WCAU TO NEW YORK'S WABC, HE WROTE OUT THIS DETAILED, SEVEN-PAGE DESCRIPTION OF THE SEQUENCE OF EVENTS.

ZACHERLE ----- BAKER SARD

CHARLES VANDA..... V.P. IN CHARGE OF TV..WCAU PHILA.
ISOBEL BAKER...... ONE TIME AGENT FOR JOHN ZACHERLE
ELLIS SARD........ FILM PRODUCER, US PRODUCTIONS NEW YORK CITY
AL BOLLANDER...... WABC TV PROGRAM DIRECTOR
ROBERT STONE...... WABCTV. STATION MANAGER ..FALL 1958
JOE STAMMLER...... WABCTV. STAION MANAGER SUCCESSOR TO MR STONE
HARRY KALSHIEM ... WM. MORRIS AGENCY
SOL RADAM......... WM MORRIS AGENCY
HAROLD BAKER...... LAWYER REPRESENTING SARD-BAKER INTEREST;(HUSBAND OF
                       ISOBEL BAKER)
THOMAS FRAME JR... LWYER REPRESENTING JOHN ZACHERLE , (PHILA, PA)
HAROLD COHEN...... ASHLEY-STEINER INC. NEW YORK CITY.
BERNIE LOWE....... CAMEO RECORDS, PHILA, PA.

        BEGINNING IN OCTOBER OF 1957 WITH THE RELEASE OF THE NOW

FAMILIAR "SHOCK THEATRE" SERIES OF MOVIES, I WAS EMPLOYED ON A WEEK

TO WEEK BASIS AT WCAU TV IN PHILA PA. AS A CHARACTER ACTOR PORTRAYING

A SOMEWHAT NUTTY MAD EXPERIMENTOR..FRIEND OF ALL MONSTERS ETC.

        NO CONTRACT WAS EVER OFFERED BY MR VANDA OF WCAU .... AND AS

THE SHOW BEGAN TO STEAMROLLER THE CITY AND THE PUBLIC RESPONSE REACHED

IT'S PEAK WITH A 12,000 ATTENDANCE FIGURE AT AN OPEN HOUSE DAY... AND

AS A RESULT OF TEAN-AGE RCORD MADE BY ME THRU BERNIE LOWE, (HAVING

NO CONTRACT FORBIDDING ME FROM RECORDING), EVENTUALLY MUCH INTEREST

WAS EXPRESSED IN THE NEW YORK AREA TO FIND OUT WHAT WAS GOING ON DOWN

IN PHILADELPHIA... I WAS ASKED TO COME TO NEW YORK AND HERE I MET WITH

ALL THE BIG AGENCIES.. WM. MORRIS BEING PARTICULARLY HELPFUL WITH

ADVICE CONCERNING AN APPEARANCE I WAS ASKED TO MAKE ON THE DICK CLARK

SHOW IN FEB.1958. (A TOUCHY SUBJECT ...WCAU NOT HAPPY WITH THE RECORD...
                OR WITH DICK CLARK...ANOTHER NETWORK)
        I DID NOT HOWEVER MAKE A MOVE TO THE NEW YORK SCENE.. INSTEAD

I REMAINED WITH THE PHILADELPHIA PRESENTATION... FINALLY SETTLING ON

THE CHOICE OF ISOBEL BAKER AS MY AGENT IN NEW YORK... MOSTLY THRU THE

RECOMMENDATION OF A FRIEND WHO KNEW HER SECRETARY AND THRU MY OWN

UNWILLINGNESS TO GET SWALLOWED UP IN ONE OF THE LARGE AGENCIES...

ZACHERLE ..... SARD-BAKER

THE CONTRACT WITH CAMEO RECORDS WAS DATED 3 FEB 1958 AND EXPIRED ONE YEAR FROM THAT DATE..(SEE COPY)

I LEFT WITH MRS BAKER A COPY OF A CINESCOPE I HAD MADE OF THE PHILADELPHIA SHOW ..SHE IN TURN THOUGHT IT HAD POSSIBILITIES AND SAID SHE WAS SHOWING IT AROUND...I LEFT IT WITH HER AND TURNED MY EFFORTS TO A VERY ACTIVE SEASON OF PERSONAL APPEARANCES IN THE PHILA AREA.

MY BEING ALLOWED TO DO PERSONAL APPEARANCES WAS THE RESULT OF THE STATIONS ATTITUDE FROM THE BEGINNING OF THE SERIES... AS A WAY FOR ME TO MAKE SOME EXTRA MONEY..SINCE THE PAY WAS ONLY 70.00 PER WEEK ... EVENTUALLY THE STAION MANAGEMENT VOICED OBJECTIONS AND ASKED FOR A SHARE IN THE P.A. MONEY WHICH I REFUSED TO GIVE...I WAS PUT OFF THE AIR FOR A WEEKEND.. DURING WHICH TIME THE PUBLIC RESPONSE WAS SOMEWHAT NOISY AND I WAS REINSTATED WITH A SLIGHT RAISE.. AND WITH THE CONTINUED FREEDOM TO GO WHERE I CHOSE AND KEEP WHAT I EARNED.

THE STATION WRITER ASSIGNED TO THE SHOW IN PHIAL.. FELT LEFT OUT OF THE FINANCIAL END OF THINGS AND THOUGH HE WAS PAID AN ADDITIONAL SUM TO WRITE THE SHOW.. HE WAS INCENSED AT THE STATION FOR NOT BEGINNING A MERCHANDISING CAMPAIGN... IN SPITE OF PROMISES THAT THEY WOULD.. EVENTUALLY HE BEGAN TO LICENSE MANUFACTURERS ON HIS OWN.. THIS BROUGHT THE RATH OF THE STATION UPON HIM... AND GENERAL UNPLEASANT RELATIONS DEVELOPED ALL AROUND....ALL THIS OCCURED DURING THE SUMMER OF 1958 AND AS THE FALL SEASON APPRAOCHED.. MRS BAKER LET ME KNOW THAT SHE HAD A MR ELLIS SARD INTERESTED IN THE SHOW AND THAT HE WAS TRYING TO PEDDLE THE IDEA HERE IN NEW YORK... HE WAS SUCCESSFUL IN FACT, AS HE ARRANGED FOR ABC NETWORK TO MAKE A CINESCOPE OF A PROJECTED HALF HOUR SERIES CALLED "TALES OF FRANKENSTEIN" WITH MYSELF AS HOST AND WITH WILDROOT AS THE SPONSOR... WILDROOT BALKED AT THE COST AND THE POOR FILM MATERIAL (AND MAYBE ME. I NEVER KNEW) I RETURNED TO PHILA

(I SEE THAT I HAVE FORGOTTEN TO MENTION THE FACT THE I GAVE
MRS BAKER AND MR SARD THE RIGHT TO REPRESENT ME ON THE 17 JUNE 1958
...MRS BAKER STILL MY AGENT AT THAT TIME...)

THE CBS NETWORK HAD PURCHASED THE STATION IN PHILA AND WAS FINALLY
GETTING READY TO MOVE IN IN SEPT OF 1958... AND LET IT BE KNOWN THAT
IT WAS THIER INTENTION TO SCHEDULT THE SHOCK MOVIES AS THE SECOND
FEATURE OF THE EVENING... A THOUGHT THAT SEEMED THEEND OF THE SHOW TO
ME..

MRS BAKER CALLED ME OVER TO NEW YORK AND SPOKE OF THE ABC LOCAL
INTEREST (CHANNEL SEVEN) ..THE NETWORK INTEREST WAS DORMANT... (A LARGE
EXCLUSIVE NETWORK CONTRACT HAD BEEN PASSED AROUND WITH MUCH EXCITEMENT
FOR A MONTH OR SO...) I WAS ACCOMPANIED BY MR. FRAME.. MY LAWYER FROM
PHILA.. AND WE WERE ASKED TO SIGN A CONTRACT WITH BAKER SARD AS PACKAGERS
OF ME... WE AGREED ONLY ON AN EXTENTION OF THE 17 JUNE AGREEMENT WITH
CERTAIN RIGHTS ADDED .. THE DRAFT DATED 14th of AUGUST 1958...(SEE COPY)

THE TERM PACKAGERS WAS EXPLAINED TO US AND IT BECAME APPARANT
THAT I WAS NOT TO HAVE A SHARE IN THE COMPANY FOR WHICH I WAS TO WORK...
ALL NEGOTIATIONS FROM THAT POINT ON WERE WITH AN INTENT ON MY PART TO
GET A SHARE OF THE PACKAGE...

IT WAS EARLY IN AUGUST THAT MRS BAKER INFORMED ME THAT SHE
HAD GIVEN UP HER AGENCY ON DOCTORS ORDERS AND THAT SHE WAS NO LONGER
MY AGENT AND SUGGESTED THAT I SHOULD GET ONE. ...I DID NOT PURSUE THAT
ADVICE AT THAT TIME, BEING EXTREMELY BUSY IN PHILA AND NEW JERSEY WITH
PERSONAL APPEARANCES AND THE SHOW ITSELF IN PHILA.. WHERE THE DIS-
ENCHANTED WRITER HAD BY THIS TIME LEFT OFF WRITING AND IT WAS LEFT
UP TO THE DIRECTOR AND MYSELF TO COME UP WITH THE SHOWS FOR AIR TIME..

BAKER AND SARD HAD BY NOW A CONTRACT FROM ABC TV IN NEW
YORK.. A VERY TIGHT AND TOUGH AFFAIR.. ABC KNOWINT THAT THEY WERE
THE SOLE OWNERS OF SHOCK MOVIES IN N.Y.C WERE NOT ABOUT TO GIVE ANY

THE CONTRACT WAS SUPPOSED TO PROVIDE ADDITIONAL MONIES FOR THE
PRODUCERS (S&B) ABOVE AND BEYOND MY SALARY.. AS PRESCRIBED BY AFTRA
AS THE MINIMUM I COULD ACCEPT...THE MAIN AND TOUGHEST PART OF THE
CONTRACT WAS THAT IT COULD BE CANCELLED WITH FOUR WEEKS NOTICE AND
THAT OPTIONS WERE GOOD FOR A TOTAL OF 39 WEEKS ENDING THE 20th OF JUNE 59.
WITH VERY LITTLE CHANCE FOR FINANCIAL INCREASE IN THE MEANTIME.

SEVERAL MEETINGS WERE HELD AT WHICH MR FRAME ACCOMPANIED ME
AND DURING WHICH WE TRIED TO GET THE OTHER PARTIES TO AGREE TO OPEN
UP THIS "PACKAGE" AS THEY CALLED IT, (ME)...HAROLD BAKER WOULD DRAW
UP A DOCUEMENT,... AND THEN WE WOULD DRAW UP OUR VERSION... BEING CAREFUL
TO AVOID EXTENDING THE RIGHTS BEYOND THE "GHOUL TYPE" CHARACTERIZATION
AND NOT MUCH BEYOND THE TV PRESENTATION....HOWEVER.. THE FINAL DAY
ARRIVED FOR SIGNING THE ABC CONTRACT FOR THE LOCAL SHOW IN NEW YORK..
AND WE STILL HAD NOT AGREED ON A CONTRACT BETWEEN OURSELVES... IN FACT
I CAME TO NEW YORK ON THAT "FINAL " DAY WITH A NEW VERSION IN HAND
... BUT IT WAS NEVER DISCUSSED... FOR MRS BAKER AT MY INSISTANCE CALLED
THE UNION (AFTRA) TO CHECK THE FIGURES THAT ABC SAID WERE CORRECT
AND FOUND THAT UNDER CERTAIN CONDITIONS ..NAMELY IF I WORKED SIX DAYS
A WEEK.. THE "PACKAGE" WOULD BE LEFT WITH FIVE DOLLARS! ...

THIS REVELATION CAUSED A MILD SENSATION AND THERE ENSUED A
VIOLENT PHONE CONVERSATION BETWEEN MR AND MRS BAKER AND MR AL HOLLANDER
OF ABC... WHO FINALLY SAID "SIGN IT OR NO SHOW."... I SIGNED AS AN
INTERESTED PARTY, OR WHATEVER THE LEGAL TERM IS.. AGREING TO ABIDE BY IT.
AND THEN I LEFT FOR PHILA.. NOT HAVING DISCUSSED OUR PACKAGE CONTRACT..

THE FIRST DAY THAT WE WERE UNDER THE ABC CONTRACT THE
PRODUCERS..(S&B) INFORMED ME THAT I WOULD BE EXPECTED TO PAY THE LIABILITY
INSURANCE FOR THEM... I OBJECTED.. AND ON THE ADVICE FROM MR FRAME
OFFERED TO PAY A THIRD OF THE COST... THEY WERE FIRM TO THE POINT OF
not yielding an inch

I THEN INFORMED MR FRAME THAT THE SITUATION WAS GETTING OUT OF
HAND AND THAT I THOUGHT A HAD BETTER LOOK UP WM MORRIS AND SEE IF THEY
WERE INTERESTED IN HELPING ME... MR HARRY KALSHEEM SAID HE WAS.. AND
GAVE ME OVER TO MR SOL RADAM.. WHO HAD A MEETING WITH HAROLD BAKER
AND CAME AWAY FROM THE MEETING SAYING THAT BAKER FELT I SHOULD BE
GRATEFUL ETC.. FOR ALL THAT THEY HAD DONE AND THAT I SHOULD SIGN
AS AN EMPLOYEE AND GET IT OVER WITH... THIS SITUATION DRAGGED ON FOR
ABOUT TWO MONTHS... WM MORRIS FIANLLY DECIDING THAT THEY WOULD ADVISE
ME BUT NOT GET INTO THE SITUATUION (ie. sign me up) WHILE THE SHOW WAS
ON A LOCAL STATION...(MR HAL COHEN HAD CALLED THE OFFICE AT ABC AND
OFFERED HIS SERVICES SHORTLY AFTER I HAD SOUGHT OUT WM MORRIS)...

THE SHOW WAS PUT ON THE AIR WITH MR SARD TAKING A VERY ACTIVE
PART .. WRITING AND PRODUCING... APPARRNTLY SHARING WITH MRS BAKER
THE PRODUCERS FEE.
                    STONE
INTRIGUE : MR STONE OF ABC TV TALKED TO ME DIRECTLY.. WHICH
MADE MR SARD FURIOUS TO SAY THE LEAST... AND ASKED ME TO DO FOUR
NIGHTS VOICE-OVER IN ADDITION TO THE TWO NIGHTS LIVE... I AGREED AS HE
SAID HE WOULD NOT DEAL WITH SARD BAKER...ON THE OCCASSION OF THE FIRST
PAY CHECK BEING WRITTEN.. MR HOLLANDER CALLED ME AND ASKED IF IT WAS
MY WISH THAT THE ENTIRE MONEY GO THROUGH THE PRODUCERS.. I TOLD HIM
IT WOULD BE HAPPIER THAT WAY... AND THIS WAS DONE.. I RECIEVED MY
MONEY FROM SARD BAKER ...AT FIRST THEY WANTED ME TO BILL THEM AS
AN INDEPENDENT CONTRACTOR TO SAVE THEM TAX MONEY... SOL RADAM ADVISED
AGAINST THIS AND I WAS PAID AS AN EMPLOYEE.

WHEN IT BECAME APPARENT THAT SOL RADAM WAS NOT GOING TO ENTER
THE FRAY WITH GUSTO.. I WAS PREVAILED UPON BY MR SARD TO TRY MR COHEN.
THIS I DID... FIANLLY SIGNING WITH ASHLEY STEINER AND HAVING MR COHEN
IN MY CORNER FROM THAT POINT ON... (DEC 4 1958). ...HE HAD SEVERAL

MEETINGS WITH MR BAKER AND WITH ABC TV IN AN ATTEMPT TO RESOLVE
THE DIFFERENCES.. AND FINALLY BROUGHT AFTRA INTO THE PICTURE AND
MR IRV LEWIS OF THE UNION EVENTUALLY PUT THE PRODUCERS ON THE UNFAIR
LIST SINCE THEY HAD BEEN ACCEPTING THE WORD OF ABCTV FOR WHAT I WAS
SUPPOSED TO RECEIVE AND NPT WHAT THE UNION SAID WAS SCALE MONEY..
AND BECAUSE THE PRODUCERS WERE CONSISTENTLY LATE IN THEIR PAYMENTS
TO ME.... ABC HAD AT LAST TO MAKE UP THE DIFFERENCE IN THE MONEY...
AND THE PRODUCERS HAVE BEEN REMOVED FROM THE UNFAIR LIST THIS FIRST
WEEK OF JULY 1959.. I HAVE IN THE MEAN TIME PAID OUT ABOUT 700.00
IN INSURANCE MONEY TO PROTECT MYSELF AS WELL AS THE PRODUCERS.. FOR
THEY APPARANTLY NEVER HAD ANY MONEY TO BACK THEMSELVES UP... AND I COULD
NOT AFFORD NOT TO BE COVERED...

        MR. SARD LET ME KNOW THAT IT WAS HIS INTENTION TO BACK OUT
WHEN THE FIRST THIRTEEN WEEKS WERE UP AND RETURN TO HIS OWN BUSINESS
.. HE WOULD HAVE DONE SO.. EXCEPT THAT THERE WAS A POSSIBLE OPNNING
FOR US ON THE NETWORK WITH THE SMMY KAYE SHOW SCHEDULED TO GO OFF
AFTER CHRISTMAS... SRAD REMANINED... BUT THE KAYE SHOW ALSO REMAINED
AND THE NETWORK OPENING DID NOT MATERIALIZE...HE FINALLY LEFT THE SCENE
AT THE ENND OF THE SECOND THIRTEEN WEEK PERIOD AND I WAS LEFT TO PRODUCE
WRITE AND ACT THE SHOW BY MYSELF... MR HOLLANDER.. ON HEARING THAT I
WAS ALONE.. HIRED A MR PAUL KINGSLEY TO HELP AS WRITER AND DEDUCTED HIS
SALARY FROM THE PRODUCERS WEEKLY PAYCHECK... MRS BAKER... THE PAYMASTER
FOR SARD BAKER.. SENT THE CHECK BACK TO MR HOLLANDER AS A BREACH OF
CONTRACT ..IN SPITE OF THE FACT THAT THE PRODUCERS WERE NO LONGER
WORKING... ABC DECIDED THAT IT WAS EASIER TO PAY THEM THE FULL AMOUNT
IN ADDITION TO PAYING MR KINGSLEY AND IN SPITE OF ADVICE FROM MR
COHEN.. CONTINUED TO DO BUSINESS WITH SARD-BAKER SIMPLY TO AVOID
A LEGAL HASSLE, APPARENTLY...

M R. BAKER HAD SENT A VERSION OF HIS IDEA OF HOW TO DISSOLVE THE ARRANGEMENTS BETWEEN US ... BUT IT TURNED OUT TO BE A RATHER BROAD DOCUEMENT AND DID NOT INSPIRE ME TO PURSUE A SETTLEMENT ON THOSE LINES.. ?.... NOW THE TIME HAS RUN OUT ON THE WHOLE WORKS... THE 39 WEEKS ARE UP... ABC HAS NO OPTION.. SARD BAKER HAVE NO OPTION... THE QUESTION REMAINS... DO SARD BAKER HAVE ANY HOLD... THERE HAS BEEN NO MERCHANDISING ..AND NO RECORD CONTRACTS.... ALSO I HAVE MADE TWO APPEARANCES DURING THE COURSE OF THE SHOW.. ONE ON THE JACK PARR SHOW IN DECEMBER OF 1958 AND ONE IN NEWARK NEW JERSEY ON THE 9th JUNE 59...

ELLIS SARD PUT IN LOTS OF TIME AND EFFORT...AND CLAIMS THAT HE WARNED MRS BAKER ABOUT HER ATTEMPTS TO "PACKAGE "ME... IN THE BEGINNING HE WAS JUST AS XXXXXXXX MUCH IN FAVOR OF THE PACKAGE AS SHE WAS... ONLY CHANGING HIS ATTITUDE WHEN HE SAW THAT I WOULD NOT SIGN... THEN HE SAID HE DID NOT CARE HOW THINGS WERE SPLIT UP... AS LONG AS HE "WAS PROTECTED AND NOT LEFT OUT IN THE COLD" AS HAD BEEN HIS EXPERIENCE BEFORE IN THE LAND OF TV.

THE SHOW HAS A BIG FOLLOWING AND IS BASICALLY THE SAME AS THE SHOW IN PHILA... THOUGH I THINK THE CHARACTER I PORTRAY IS SOMEWHAT NUTTIER AND THERE IS THE ADDED FEATURE OF THE ABC MUSICIANS THAT HAS GIVEN THE SHOW ANOTHER DIMENSION...THE FORMAT HAS BEEN COPIED BY SEVERAL STATIONS AROUND THE COUNTRY... WITH THEIR OWN TYPE OF GHOUL DOING THE NONSENSE AT INTERMISSION TIME..

SARD HAS BEEN ACTIVE TRYING TI GET INTEREST ON OTHER STATIONS.. ACTUALLY HAS BEEN GETTING IN THE WAY OF MR COHEN....AND HAS GONE SO FAR AS TO JOIN A GROUP KNOWN AS THE PICKWICKS WHO HAVE SOME SORT OF VARIETY FORMAT IN MIND... HE HAS TOLD ME REPEATEDLY THAT HE HAS BROKEN OFF WITH MRS BAKER.. AND THAT THE BOOKS OF THIER CORPORATION ARE CLOSED.

ON THE FOLLOWING PAGES YOU'LL FIND ZACH'S CONTRACT WITH WABC-TV, THE NEW YORK TV STATION THAT MADE HIM THEIR RESIDENT HORROR HOST.

DRAFT

THIS AGREEMENT , made this 14th day of August 1958 between John K. Zacherle
(Herein afterwards referred to as Mr. Zacherle)
of 10 Grove Ave., Flourtown Penna.,and Isobel Baker and Ellis Sard

of New York ,(Herein afterwards referred to as the Packagers) .

WITNESSETH

WHEREAS.- on June 17, 1958 Mr Zacherle appointed and continued the appointment of
the packagers as his exclusive representatives TO AND INCLUDING OCT 2 1958, IN
NEGOTIATING FOR A TELEVISION PROGRAM FEATURING MR ZACHERLE IN A GHOUL TYPE CHARACTERI-
ZATION AND THE PACKAGERS AS SUCH REPRESENTATIVES HAVE CONDUCTED NEGOTIATIONS WITH ABC-TV
AND OTHERS TO THE PROMOTION OF MR ZACHERLE'S TALENTS ON SUCH A TV SHOW AND

WHEREAS THE PACKAGERS ARE ABOUT TO ENTER INTO AN AGREEMENT WITH WABC-TV N.Y.
WHICH AGREEMENT PROVIDES THAT THE PACKERS SHALL MAKE AVAILABLE TO WABC TV THE SERVICES
OF MR. ZACHERLE ON A SERIES OF WEEKLY TV PROGRAMS UNDER CONDITIONS SET FORTH THEREIN
AND

WHEREAS MR. ZACHERLE HAS READ SAID PROPOSED AGREEMENT AND APPROVES THEREOF,
AND FOR THE PURPOSES OF ENABLING THE PACKAGERS TO CARRY OUT ALL OF THE TERMS AND
CONDITIONS WITH WABC TV , WISHES TO ENTER INTO A SEPERATE AGREEMENT WITH THE PACKAGERS,
GRANTING TO THEM THE EXCLUSIVE USE OF HIS SERVICES HEREIN MENTIONED, TOGETHER WITH
CERTAIN EXCEPTIONS HEREIN MENTIONED, AND THE RIGHT THE RIGHT TO EXPLOIT HIS NAME
AND TALENTS DURING THE PERIOD WHEN SUCH AGREEMENT WITH THE PACKAGERS IS IN FULL
FORCE AND EFFECT.

THE MUTUAL
NOW THEREFORE , IN CONSIDERATION OF THE PREMISES AND COVANENTS HEREIN CONTAINED,
THE PARTIES HERETO AGREE AS FOLLOWS:

1. MR. ZACHERLE AGREES TO RENDER HIS SERVICES TO THE PACKAGERS AS A PER-
FORMER ON A SERIES OF WEEKLY TV PROGRAMS FOR THE PERIOD ENDING DEC. 31,1958 and at THE
ELECTION OF THE PACKAGERS, FOR AN ADDITIONAL THIRTEEN WEEKS THEREAFTER, DURING WHICH

PERIOD AS SPECIFIED, THE PACKAGERS SHALL HAVE THE EXCLUSIVE RIGHT TO NEGOTIATE WITH ABC OR ANY OTHER NETWORK OR STATION, FOR THE USE OF MR. ZACHERLE'S SERVICES IN SIMILAR PROGRAMS, AND ACCORDING TO THE TERMS AND PROVISIONS OF SUCH CONTRACTS AS THEY MAY ENTER INTO, SUBJECT TO THE APPROVAL OF MR. ZACHERLE, WHICH APPROVAL SHALL NOT BE UNREASONABLY WITHHELD.

2. ANY MONEYS DERIVED FROM THE SALE/AND OR LICENSING OF ALL SUBSIDIARY MARKETING, MERCHANDISING, AND EXPLOITATION RIGHTS INCLUDING ROYALTIES FROM RECORDS SHALL BE DIVIDED AS BETWEEN THE PACKAGERS AND MR. ZACHERLE IN THE PROPORTION OF 60 % TO MR. ZACHERLE AND 40 % TO THE PACKAGERS.

IT IS UNDERSTOOD THAT THE EXCLUSIVE SERVICES OF MR. ZACHERLE REFERRED TO HEREIN ARE SUBJECT TO HIS PRESENT APPEARANCES ON SHOCK THEATRE OVER WCAU TV IN PHILADELPHIA, AND SUCH RIGHTS AS MAY BE PRESENTLY OUTSTANDING UNDER A CERTAIN AGREEMENT WITH CAMEO RECORDS , DATED 3 FEBRUARY 1958 , AND PERSONAL APPEARANCES FOR WHICH ARRANGEMENTS AHVE BEEN MADE PRIOR TO THE DATE OF THIS AGREEMENT. HEREAFTER SUCH PERSONAL APPEARANCES AS MAY BE UNDERTAKEN BY MR. ZACHERLE SHALL BE WITH THE PRIOR APPROVAL OF THE PACKAGERS.

3. NO ASSIGNMENT OTHER THAN ONE MADE BY THE PACKAGERS TO A SUCCEEDING CORPORATION IN WHICH THEY SHALL RETAIN CONTROL OF THIS OR OF ANY OTHER RIGHT OR INTEREST HEREIN, SHALL BE VALID UNLESS THE WRITTEN CONSENT OF THE OTHER PARTY HERETO BE OBTAINED IN ADVANCE OF THE MAKING OF SUCH ASSIGNMENT.

4. MR. ZACHERLE REPRESENTS AND WARRANTS, SUBJECT TO THE EXCEPTIONS ABOVE, REFERRING TO HIS APPEARANCE IN HIS SHOW SHOCK THEATRE NOW BEING TELEVISED OVER STATION WCAU TV IN PHILA., AND SUCH RECORDING RIGHTS AS CAMEO RECORDS OF PHILA. MAY HAVE PURSUANT TO THE AGREEMENT WITH MR. ZACHERLE DATED 3 FEBRUARY 1958, AND FURTHER SUBJECT TO SUCH COMMITTMENTS WHICH MR. ZACHERLE MAY HAVE MADE FOR PERSONAL APPEARANCES PRIOR TO THE DATE HEREOF, THAT HE HAS THE RIGHT AND POWER TO ENTER INTO AND PERFORM THIS AGREEMENT.

IN WITNESS WHEREOF , THE PARTIES HERETO HAVE SET THEIR HANDS AND SEALS THE DAY AND YEAR FIRST WRITTEN.

WITNAESS   JOHN K. ZACHERLE

                            ISOBEL BAKER

                            ELLIS SARD

ON THE NEXT TWO PAGES ARE ZACH'S HANDWRITTEN NOTES FOR HIS HOSTING OF 1933'S *NIGHT OF TERROR* (ON OCTOBER 3, 1958) AND 1940'S *BEFORE I HANG* (ON JANUARY 2, 1959). IN THE LATTER EPISODE, ZACH'S GIANT AMOEBA (OR, IN LATIN, "SLOBBUS AMOEBUS") MADE ITS FIRST NEW YORK APPEARANCE.

THEY'RE FOLLOWED BY ZACH'S NOTES FOR A *BRIDE OF FRANKENSTEIN*-INSPIRED SHOW WHERE HE CREATED A BRIDE FOR GASPORT, AND AN ASSORTMENT OF HANDWRITTEN, HALF-CENTURY-OLD NOTES WITH OTHER SHOW IDEAS.

notes on
" Night of Terror "

Acting awards.

- Burial equipment
- "Burial when she's wedding"

- My sister in this dramatization
  (I told her not to go into the
  acting game)
- sister goes into Trance.

- Director of this pix trying to kill
  off all the actors.

- "Bela says" I forbid it, I forbid it!"
- scearce
- sister killed before last break

- Oriental cigarittes (candy?)
- young boob shows how he got
  out of box.

- "Police inspector a nut"

Best Stuff

Uni-cell - Ameoba

(disconnected sections of spaghetti - no central "clearing house" - so it never moves - just sits

Nervous system

eats plankton DUST

digestive system

eats — whorls - spider eggs can eat from any side of body - suction action

serum producing area

serum used as hair restorer?

or ??

burned out bulb

plungers to be worked from below for talking, eating or heartbeat effect

(perhaps pour some bubble liquid for Lawrence Welk effect)

- Air hose for f bubble effect. (talking?)

- Ameoba can't perspire thru skin like a dog - but has no tongue so is under constant strain in hot weather & stores all its nervous energy in the serum section

136

"Bride of Gasport" #2.

- using small "mummy" dolls
- sent in
- diathermy machine
- Bride of Frankenstein effects

(like Praetorius dolls)

① place mouse heart into smallest mummy or stick mummy in "tana leaf smoke box" to get heart beating
    check heart - sound effect - meter
    etc - (cha cha beat?)
    check Gasports heart rythm
      (compatable personalities)

② put Gasport at one end of table and doll at other - wire heads together

to get the mummy (wife) in
       the right →

frame of mind to fall in love w/ gas.
(machine shorts out)

3.

set Diathermy machine on end and

Gasport

turn on juice (turn doll's head)

after Commercial doll is larger and
smoking all over (bottled smoke) (otherwise
known as "McNally's Threat")
Gasport is panting with anticipation
put doll in a burlap sack so Gasport
won't feel selfconscious when he finally
sees her.

(4.) send yanoush up to pull up
the kite (big storm stuff)

   Z gets shock from premature lightning ~~bolt~~ bolt
        pix to negative
after commercial

   tell yanoush to haul away —
   Gasport goes up — doll stays
   down — big mix up. —

   big thunder & lightning — Gasport
        falls down lands on Z.

(5.) all set — generator noises etc.
lightning hits ~~on~~ flash pot —
smoke powder — McNally wallos out
of control room —
   after commercial the burlap sacks
are facing each other on table

And I opens each sack so that
they can "kill each other —
   Gasport is terrified — And
jumps off table (yanked by Stoney)

   I thinks Mrs Gasport is kinda cute
and big arguement started by Isabel.

   <u>Close</u> — big family fight —

   I agrees to take Mrs. Gasport
to meet Larry

   Brilliant work!

   Peobody Award!

— give Gaspert a bath!

— Gaspert ~~Medi. check-up~~

— Diathermy machine.

— "foaming unknown".

— Transyl. rating machine.

— Safety show

— Party for som. body.

— wiring.

— Invisible demonstration.
            (long underwear.)

— build monster.

— "demonstrate how to movie"
      make-up my dear,
      false teeth clap stick
      her premiere performance.
      Gaspert blows it all up

~~Go Shrink rays~~

~~Voodoo Doll~~

—

Lie Detectar + brains

—

Flying abject

—

Dig tunnel

—

Anti Gravity.

—

2nd Moon shoat

— Giant Spider web.

— ~~Straight jacket~~

spare-rib bank.

heart bank.
(use heart as a pump, (with hearts to
gut.)

Amoeba covered w/ ~~the~~ gauze to hold its shape
eye (light bulb)
at each end?
(spaghetti nerve)

inject it — to make it ~~multiply~~ or to make a screen
- do a quick nerve transplant on it
- falls on floor + divides

Art show

experiment:
work on a sponge

IDEAS (?)

- Try to get Gasport out of sack (Psycho).
- Build giant calculator by hooking up a bunch of brains
- Lecture on growing hair
- " on how to raise ▓▓▓
- Brain transplant (soapy foam?)
- History of Transylvanian language. Pig German - French. "Berlitz" record
- Isabel gets sick (Bubbles) — cure.
- Nervous system lecture w/spaghetti
- Normal skull - small skeleton.

ZACK EATS TANNA LEAVES & swells. (The heck he does!)

"amoeba patticakes"

— they get all steamed
up
(lots of noise
steam, etc.)

perhaps
we could
make 1/2 doz
small ones

on strings
that
would
jump all
over the table

— acts like things are out
of control at
"swats" them

bedlam

Sat. ("Thursday)   Reptile

Moho-ing / scientific project
                     to probe center of
                              earth.

          aut inaccum —
             ridiculous

I've been down before.
           check axis
headstart at my depth —

①

Zach's notes for his episode on the "Moho Project,"
in which he began digging to the center of the Earth.
The film that night (May 2, 1959) was The Man
Who Lived Twice *(1936) with Ralph Bellamy.*

(2.) — one more bomb
        just to celebrate
        the day after May day

— Tripod —
        discus shape of worth

Ora 47
mass   who cares
beams lift
        rope - pulley pail
        ~~plumbers~~
add skateline

Toss in gasport.
                do digging.

                        gasport
                        shatters
                        ash falls
                        out of
                        hiring
                        grabs rope.
                        end up taut
                        afright

"good luck young lady"

③ Back comes up all dusty.

unstraps off,

hoist signal bell —

— retrieves, —

— sand & water. (just bite it)

(Later) (Parliament) glob of dough recognize —
1/4" (pressurized
feedback sea water)
salt squeezed
out.

leaky faucets no problem
— moves too
slow.

out of faucet.
cut off some
water
chew it.

ON THE NEXT 35 PAGES ARE ZACH'S SCRIPTS FOR THREE OF HIS WOR SHOWS. NONE IS BASED ON WHATEVER MOVIE WAS PLAYING THAT NIGHT. THEY'RE FOLLOWED BY ONE OF HIS WACKY PROP LISTS.

```
THEME                              (ZACH IN CHAIR READING BOOK)

                         JUST READING HISTORY OF DR. FRANKENSTEIN...

                         TIME HE LEFT TRANS AND TOOK TRIP TO RUSSIA.

                         GRAND CHAP....COULDN'T STAND THE PEASANTS

                         THOUGH....DIDN'T LIKE THEM THROWING ROCKS

                         AT HIM....VERY SELF CONCSIOUS....

                            WROTE A LITTLE OPERA ABOUT TRIP...

                         ..PREFORMED HERE FIRST TIME...DEAR WIFE

                         AT KEYS....GRAND REVIEWS ABOUT LAST ONE...

S.E. ISOBEL              .. YES MY DEAR....ANXIOUS TO GET STARTED

                         BEEN PRACTICING ALL WEEK....

                            GRAND OLD TRANS. DELEGATION HERE...FROM

                         EMBASSY....  GREAT BUNCH OF BOYS......

S.E.  DISORDERLY MOB     ALL RIGHT UP THERE LETS QUIET DOWN....

   UP AND OUT            .... EVERYBODY SIT DOWN....I'LL THROW YOU

S.E.  HISSES,BOOS        ALL OUT..... (JUNK THROWN AT ZACH......DUCK)

                         LET'S HAVE NONE OF THAT....LITTLE RESTLESS..

                         ..BOB KENNEDY WANTS THEM DEPORTED....UNDESIR*

                         ABLE ALIENS.....

                            FIRST ACT COMING UP HERE....DR. FRANK AND

                         FRANKIE LEAVE TRANS...HEAD FOR RUSSIA....

                         ..PICKED UP BY SECRET POLICE....DR. FRANK

                         DEMANDS TO SEE KRUSCH.....GO TO KREMLIN...

                         ...SING "EL MONSTERO EL KRUSCHEVIO"...(MONSTERS

                         FOR KRUSCH) ....ALL RIGHT DEAR...GET W/ IT

(OH SUSANNA)            OH I COME FROM TRANS. AND I'VE BROUGHT MY
                                MONSTER TOO
                         WE'RE HERE TO RAID YOUR GRAVEYARDS AND
                                EXPERIMENT W/YOU
```

                    WE'LL DO OUR BEST TO HELP YOU SIR IF
                        YOU WILL LET US GO
                    WE'LL KILL OFF ALL THE PEASANTS AND A
                        CAPATILIST OR SO

        CH.   OH NIKITA, WE'LL CHASE AWAY YOUR BLUES
                    WE'LL MAKE LOTS OF MONSTERS, AND LOTS OF
                        VODKA TOO

                    OH WE'LL BUILD A BETTER MONSTER THAN THE
                        USA CAN DO
                    AND THEN BESIDES THE MISSLE RACE, YOU'LL
                        LEAD IN MONSTERS TOO
                    WE'LL MAKE HIM OUT OF ODDS AND ENDS
                    WE'LL HAVE IT READY SOON
                    WE'LL PUT HIM IN A SPUTNIK AND SHOOT HIM TO
                        THE MOON

                    REPEAT CH.

S.E. LOUD APPLAUSE   FIRST INTERMISSION....GRAND OLD MOVIE...

                    ...CREAM OF THE CROP....GREAT EXPENSE TO

                    GET IT....

                        ALL RIGHT EBERLE...ROLL THE MESS

    BREAK ONE

                    WELL, AFTER THEY CONVINCE K. THAT RUSSIA

                        NEEDS MONSTERS... LEAVE KREMLIN....LOOK

                    FOR OLD CASTLE....DR. FRANK FINDS

                    ONE...OUTSKIRTS OF MOSCOW,,,STARTS

                    LITTLE BUSINESS....MINOR BRAIN SURGERY..

                    BUILDS MONSTERS IN SPARE TIME.....

                        ONE DAY ...DO IT YOURSELF MONSTER

                    BUILDER BRINGS IN DAMAGED MONSTER....DR FRANK

                    ASKS HIM WHAT HAPPENS...HE SINGS

                        "DIE MONSTER IST KAPUTEN" (THE MONSTER
                        ISX SICK)

    (CAMPTOWN RACES) MY MONSTER IS NOT FEELING FIT, DR. DR.
                        HE FELL INTO A SULFUR PIT AND SHRUNK A
                            FOOT OR SO
                        HIS BONES ARE BROKE HIS HAIR IS SINGED
                            DR. DR.

```
                    HE LOOKS LIKE HE'S BEEN ON A BINGE
                         FIX HIM UP FOR ME

              CH.)  SCALPEL, SUTURE, SAW
                    USE THEM ALL AND MORE
                    CUT XXXXXX AND SEW HIM UP AGAIN
                    DON'T WORRY HE'S INSURED

              HIS HEART HAS STOPPED , HIS BRAINS NOT
                         RIGHT, DR. DR.
              WE HAVE TO RAID THE GRAVES TONIGHT
                         FIX HIM UP FOR ME
              PLEASE PLUG HIM IN AND CHARGE HIS BRAIN
                         DR. DR.
              WE HAVE TO MAKE AN EARLY TRAIN
                         FIX HIM UP FOR ME

              REPEAT CH.
```

S.E. APPLAUSE
      UP AND OUT   THANK YOU...THANK YOU...TOUCHING PIECE

S.E. RAZZ W/DUCK CALL   (LOOK HURT) ALL RIGHT EBERLE...KNOCK IT

                                   OFF...NO APPRECIATION OF TALENT...

                                       AFTER DR. FRANK FIXES MONSTER...

                                     WORD GETS AROUND HE'S AN EXPERT....ALL

                                   THE PEOPLE START BUILDING MONSTERS...

                                   ...ANYWHERE THEY CAN...BATHTUBS...CELLARS

                                   ...KITCHENS....THEY ALL WANT TO BE A

                                   TWO MONSTER FAMILY....K REALIZES GREAT

                                   DANGER...ORDERS ALL MONSTER BUILDING

                                   STOPPED....ALL MONSTERS KILLED...PEOPLE

                                   DON'T LIKE IT... FORM MILITIA....DR.

                                   FRANKENSTEIN HEADS IT... MONSTER UNDERGROUND

                                   MAKES PROPAGANDA MOVIES AND SHOW THEM ON T.V.

-----COMMERCIAL-----

                                   NEEDLESS TO SAY....THEY DIDN'T WORK...

                                   ...THEY RESORT TO VIOLENT MEANS....PREPARE

                                   TO STORM KREMLIN....DR. FRANK LEADS THE

                                   MARCH....GRAND TIME HAD BY ALL

BREAK TWO

                    MILITIA STORMS KREMLIN.....K DUCKS OUT

                    BACK DOOR.....HEADS FOR SIBERIA....

                    PASSES BY FRANKENSTEIN'S CASTLE....FRANKIE

                    MOWING THE LAWN.....WALKS OVER TO HIM

                        ...SINGS "ADIOSO KRUSCHEVIO"(GOODBYE K.)

(RED RIVER VALLEY)

                    FROM THE KREMLIN THEY SAY YOU ARE GOING
                    WE WILL MISS YOUR BALD HEAD AND SWEET SMILE
                    THEY ALL SAY YOU ARE TAKING OUR MONEY
                    TO BUILD A MOTEL ON THE NILE
                    WON'T YOU THINK OF THE COUNTRY YOU'RE LEAVING
                    OH HOW LONELY AND SAD WHEN YOU GO
                    WON'T YOU THINK OF THE COMM. PARTY
                    IF YOU'RE GOING YOU'RE RUNNING TOO SLOW

                    AFTER SONG...FRANKIE CHASES AFTER HIMX ..

                        ...STRAIGHT TO SIBERIA...K. LIVES

                    HAPPILY....MAKING ONE MINUTE ART FILMS...

                ----COMMERCIAL----

                    AFTER THE REVOLUTION...PEOPLE ELECT DR.

                    FRANK PREMIER.....IMMEDIATELY OUTLAWS

                    COMM. PARTY....REPLACES IT W/WEREWOLF PARTY..

                        ..DECLARES MONSTER BUILDING NAT'L SPORT..

                    ....ALL THE TIME THOUGH, FRANKIE VERY

                    LONELY....WANTS TO GET MARRIED...RAISE FAMILY

                    ...DR. FRANK TOO BUSY TO BUILD HIM A WIFE

                    ...TOURS COUNTRY LOOKING FOR SHE-MONSTER..

                        ...

BREAK THREE

                    ONE NIGHT DR. FRANK WANTS TO RAID

                        GRAVEYARD....LOOKS FOR FRANKIE...NOT HOME

DR. F. WAITS UP FOR HIM....

...FRANKIE STAGGERS IN AT TWO O CLOCK

...THEY HEAD FOR GRAVEYARD...DR. F.

SINGS " NETSIO EL CELEBRATSIO" (WHAT HAVE

YOU BEEN CELEBRATING?)

(BILLY BOY)

OH WHERE HAVE YOU BEEN FRANKIE BOY
                              "   "
OH WHERE HAVE YOU BEEN DARLING FRANKIE
YOU HAD SOME WORK TO DO, ROBBING GRAVES
        AND COFFINS TOO
I'M AN OLD MAN AND CAN NOT DO THE DIGGING

2) GRAB A SHOVEL AND DIG FRANKIE BOY
                            "   "
    GRAB A SHOVEL AND DIG DARLING FRANKIE
    WE NEED BODIES DON'T YOU SEE
    HERE'S A GRAVE MARKED EBERLE
    HE'S A FAT ONE AND FUNNING LOOKING TOO

S.E. RAZZ W/ DUCK CALL

    RAZZ AGAIN   SING) AND FUNNY LOOKING TOO (RAZZ)

    RAZZ   ...FUNNY LOOKING.....   "

                        (LAFF) CAUGHT YOU BOY....(LAFF)

S.E. SIREN, SCREACHING
    TIRES, WHISTLES   (LOOK ALARMED) OH OH....(YELL) BEAT IT

                        BOYS....ITS KENNEDY....(DUCK BEHIND COFFIN)

                        (PICK UP RIFLE...SHOOT OFF CAMERA)

                        (LAFF) GOT'M ...I'LL HOLD THEM

FLASH POT BEHIND COFFIN   OFF BOYS....OUT THE BACK WAY

                        (FLASH POT OFF) (COUGH....TO MOVIE)

            BREAK FOUR

                    ALL THIS TIME, AS XX I SAID...FRANKIE

                    LOOKING FOR WIFE...VERY UNHAPPY....

                    HE COULD HAVE HAD MINE...FREE (LAFF)

S.E ISOBEL
                ONLY FOOLING DEAR

155

FRANKIE TELLS DR. FRANK. HE WANTS TO BE

A GYPSY.....HE SINGS "NO GHOULEO EL

FRANKIO" (NO GHOUL FOR FRANKIE)

HIT IT DEAR ....(NOTHING HAPPENS)

....DEAR!............(PICK UP PAIL OF

WATER.....DUMP IN COFFIN)

S.E. SLURPING   (ZACH ..LOOK ANNOYED)

GET WITH IT DEAR...

(I DON'T WANT TO PLAY IN YOUR YARD)

I DON'T WANT TO BE A MONSTER
IT'S NO FUN TO BE A JERK
YOU GET ALL THE FUN AND MONEY
I DO ALL THE DIRTY WORK
EVERYBODY HATES A MONSTER
EVEN LITTLE CHILDREN CRY
XXXXXXXXXXX IF YOU DON'T MAKE ME A GYPSY
I'LL HIT YOU RIGHT BETWEEN THE EYES

I'D RATHER BE A WANDERING GYPSY
BACK IN TRAN SYL VAN IX A
I'LL GET MYSELF A FEMALE GYPSY
AND THEN I'LL MARRY UP WITH HER
EVERYBODY HATES A MONSTER
EVEN LITTLE CHILDREN CRY
IF YOU DON'T MAKE ME A GYPSY
I'LL SOCK YOU RIGHT BEWTEEN THE EYES

DR. FRANK. TELLS FRANKIE ...NO BETTER

LIFE THAN A MONSTER'S...DIGGING UP GRAVES...

...CHASING PEASANTS....HE TAIKS HIM OUT

OF BECOMING A GYPSY....

COMMERCIAL

S.E. CAR SCREACHING TO STOP

(LETTER TIED TO ROCK...THROWN ON STAGE)

OH,..WAIT JUST A MINUTE HERE....GRAND NEWS

...(PICK UP PARER) ...HAPPY TO ANNOUNCE

RESULTS OF TRANS. PRIMARY....VOTES ALL COUNT-
ED....

S.E.-LOW APPLAUSE

ZACHERELY......TWO MILLION FOUR THOUSAND
AND TWENTY ONE(SMILE)

S.E. - APPLAUSE

GASPORT....TEN THOUSAND THREE HUNDRED AND
FOURTEEN ......ALL HIS
RELATIVES

OH...WAIT JUST A MINUTE(LOOK INDIGNANT)

NOW JUST A MINUTE HERE...WHAT'S THIS?

S.E. - LOUD APPLAUSE

PAT BOONE.....FIFTEEN MILLION SEVEN HUNDRED
AND EIGHTY THOUSAND FIVE HUNDRED
AND FOURTY TWO

(RIP UP PAPER)   ALL FIXED....HIS NAME

WASN'T EVEN ON THE BALLOT.....I'LL CALL

UP THE PRIME MINISTER....HIS DOING...

...YOU WATCH THE MOVIE...O.K. YARNUSH

ROLL IT BOY....

BREAK FIVE

THINGS ARE GOING ALONG JUST SWELL...

DR. FRANK HAVING GREAT TIME....THEN ONE

DAY PEOPLE FIND OUT HE'S BEEN DIPPING INTO

TILL....CALL OUT MILITIA AGAIN...MARCH

TO CASTLE....DR. FRANK SEES THEM COMING ..

..TELLS FRANKIE HE'S GOING OUT FOR TANNA

JUICE....LEAVES HIM HOLDING THE BAG...

S.E.   GASPORT CRYING

NO OFFENSE MEANT BOY......THE MOB BREAKS

DOWN THE DOOR....SEES FRANKIE....OVERWHELMED

WITH HIM.....MAKE **HIM** THE NEW PREMIER...

....DR. FRANK HITCHES RIDE TO TRANS....

HOPING PEASANTS WILL LET HIM BACK IN

...SINGS "EL TRANS. EL BACKIO" (I'M

GOING BACK TO TRANS)

(SHE'LL BE COMIN' ROUND THE MOUNTAIN)

I AM GOING BACK TO TRAN SYL VAN I A
 REPEAT
ALL THE WEREWOLVES BATS AND MUMMIES
AND ALL MY OTHER CHUMMIES
DON'T YOU WORRY I AM COMING, I'LL BE THERE

I AM GOING HOME TO TRAN SYL VAN I A
REPEAT
I'LL BE NICE TO ALL THE PEASANTS
AND I'LL EVEN BUY THEM PRESENTS
IF THEY'LL LET ME BACK IN
          TRAN SYL VAN I A

I AM HOMESICK FOR OLD TRAN SYL VAN I A
REPEAT
I WILL LEAD A BETTER LIFE
I WON'T EVEN BEAT MY WIFE
 IF THEY LET BACK IN TRAN SYL VAN I A

S.E. PHONE RINGING   HE MAKES IT BACK TO TRANS. (PHONE RINGS)

JUST A MINUTE HERE (PICK UP PHONE)

HELLO...WHO?....OH IT'S YOU KENNEDY...

....WHAT DO YOU MEAN YOU'RE GOING TO LOCK

ME UP....WE'LL JUST SEE ABOUT THAT ....

.... GO OUT AND FIND THE GUYS WHO

BROKE INTO MY CAR....(SLAM DOWN RECIEVER)

AS I WAS SAYING BEFORE I WAS INTERUPPTED..

... DR. FRANK GOES BACK TO TRANS...OPENS

UP USED CAR LOT....M*A*KES MONSTERS ON THE SIDE..

.. FRANKIE DOSN'T MAKE OUT TO WELL THOUGH..

.....KRUSH COME BACK...MOTEL DIDN'T MAKE OUT

TO GOOD....FRANKIE EXILED TO SIBERIA...

MAKES ICECUBES FOR K.'S VODKA PARTIES

THEME IN   ZACH AT COFFIN

          TONIGHT TRANSYLVANIAN FOLLIES OF 1960...

          ..SIMILAR TO VAUDEVILLE....ONLY BETTER..

          TRADITION IN TRANS...PRESENTED BY BAND

          OF GYPSIES...GREAT FEATS OF MAGIC..DANCING

          MUSIC...ACROBATICS...

            ISOBEL FORMER STAR....GREAT SHOWMAN..

          ONE ACT SHE DOES VERY WELL....DOES IT EVERY

          YEAR...GETS SAWED IN HALF....ONLY TONIGHT

          USE REAL SAW (LAFF)

          GREAT LEGEND BEHIND FOLLIES...ALL STARTED

          WHEN CROWN PRINCE WANTED TO FIND WIFE....

          SENT OUT NOTICE....ALL MAIDENS OF TRANS

          COME TO CASTLE...PREFORM THEIR ACT...BEST

          PREFORMER GETS TO MARRY PRINCE....ALL MAIDENS

          CAME...DID STUFF.....LAST ACT WAS TRICK

          SHOOTING....GIRL ASKED FOR HELPERS....ALL

          OTHER GIRLS WANTED TO IMPRESS PRINCE....ALL

          OBLIGED AND HELPED OUT GIRL....SHE WAS LOUSY

          SHOT ...BUT WON CONTEST..(LAFF)...LIVED

          HAPPILY UNTIL THE GIRL PREFORMED THE TRICK

          FOR COMPANY....USING PRINCE...(LAFF)

          EVERY YEAR WE DON GAY APPAREL...PREFORM FOLLIES..

          ...MEMORY OF PRINCE....

            LOT TO DO BEFORE START...ARRANGE ACTS...

          ...CHECK OUT DEAR WIFE & GASPORT...

S.E. MOB   GREAT BUNCH HERE TONIGHT...JUDGE CONTEST..

          ...MAKE IT REALISTIC.....WINNER GETS TO KISS

          ISOBEL...RUNNER UP GETS TONIGHTS FILM.....

EVERY GLORIOUS FOOT OF IT....BOOBY

PRIZE.....EXPECTING THE PRESS HERE...

..WRITE UP IN PAPERS...BACK IN TRANS..

HAVE SYSTEM CALLED MONEYOLLA...SLIP

BOYS FEW BUCKS...GET GOOD RIGHT UP...

S.E. MOB UP& OUT NONE OF THAT HERE... PRESS JUST ARRIVED..

..WINCHEL...BEN HECT ...ALL THE BOYS...

..HELP W/JUDGING....

BREAK ONE

ZACH BY COFFIN
SAW IN HAND

 SAW ALL SET....ISOBEL IN GRAND SHAPE..

..INSURANCE ALL PAID UP....TAKE NO

CHANCES....TRANS GYPSY BAND W/ US...

..SUPPLY MUSIC....MUST FOR ACT.....

...UNDER DIRECTION OF COUNT APRILE...

...GET BOYS READY....

S.E. FANFARE TRANS. FOLLIES 1960 PRESENTS

ZACH AND ISOBEL....PREFORMING GREAT

FEAT OF MAGIC....SAW IN HALF WITHOUT

A SCRATCH....(WAIT FOR APPLAUSE...GET NONE

PROCEED W/ACT)

 BUNCH OF NUTS UP THERE....DON'T KNOW

GREAT ACT IF IT HITS THEM....

S.E. SCREAMS AFTER
 EACH STROKE
 (PLACE SAW IN COFFIN)

(STROKE).....TICCLISH.....

 " ......DIFFERENT SPOXT

S.E. GASPORT LAUGHING ..GETTING GASPORT WORRIED...

OH....HE LIKES IT....

             (STROKE) THINGS NOT GOING WELL....

        ...(PEEK IN COFFIN).....LITTLE MESSY...

        ...WIFE NOT IN PRACTICE...BEEN WHOLE

        YEAR....NO SIGN OF LIFE....SUREFIRE

        TEST TO SEE IF ISOBEL O.K......

        (RAISE VOICE) ....HELLO THERE MR. BOONE

S.E. SCREAMS   WORKS ALL THE TIME....BIG ROMANCE GOING.

        ...SNEAKS OUT AT NIGHT...MUST BE GOING

        OUT WITH HIM....TRY AGAIN.....

        (STROKE).....LAST TIME EVER DO THAT

        ACT...ISOBEL SCREAMS TO GET VOTES....

        ...NOT FAIR.... (PEEK IN COFFIN)

        DOESN'T LOOK GOOD AT ALL....NORMAL

        FOR HER...(LAFF)

COMMERCIAL

SWORDS,BASKET   AFTER SAW TRICK....ALWAYS PREFORM

        FAMOUS SWORD IN BASKET TRICK....ALWAYS GETS

        BIG HAND....FAVORITE OF TRANS. GYPSIES...

S.E. SCREAMS   USE ISOBEL AGAIN (S.E.) DOESN'T FEEL

        UP TO IT.....WONDER WHO TO USE (PEEK AT GASP?)

GASPORT PULLED OFFSTAGE   NOTHING BUT A COWARD...LAST TIME USED HIM,

        IN HOSPITAL FOR WEEK....NO WAY FOR HIM TO

        ACT....HE CAN TRUST ME....NO CONFIDENCE IN

        OLD ZACH....HAVE TO USE STRATEGY....

        (RAISE VOICE)...LOOK AT ALL THESE NICE

GASPORT THROWN ON STAGE   JUICY FAT SPIDERS.. .

        WORKS ALL TIME....ONE WEAKNESS...SPIDERS.

        ...LOVES THEM....DO ANYTHING FOR ONE...

                    GET BASKET READY...BORROW DEAR WIFE'S

                    WASHBASKET....ALLRIGHT DEAR?????.....

                    ...(RAISE VOICE) COME ON IN PAT....

S.E. SCREAMS   (LAFF)....NEVER FAILS....

                    GASPORT GETS IN BASKET....I PUT SWORDS

                       THROUGH.....(PICK UP SWORD)...GREAT

                    STORY BEHIND THESE....HANDED DOWN BY UNCLE

                    ..FOUGHT IN TRANS. REVOLUTION....HUNG HIM

                    WHEN HE DESERTED....

                       (PUT GASPORT IN)   FIRST SWORD IN....

S.E. GROANS   ..TAKING IT JUST FINE....REALLY DOESN'T HURT..

                    ...VOTE GETTING TACTICS.....GOT IT FROM

                    ISOBEL...TEACHES HIM NASTY TRICKS...HER

                    MOTHER'S SIDE FAMILY...(IN W/ SWORD)

                    NO SIGN OF LIFE....USE TEST....DROP IN

                    SPIDER....(OPEN LID...DROP IN SPIDER)

                    NO REACTION....BAD SIGN.....HAVE TO FIND

                    SOMEONE TO HELP W/ACT....(SMILE) EBERLE??????.

S.E. DOOR SLAMS   COWARD....NO HELP AT ALL...(THROW BASKET

                    ON FLOOR).....CAN'T USE GASPORT....ALL SHOCK

                    UP...NEVER BE SAME AGAIN....

S.E. LAUGHING   MUST HAVE RECOVERED. .HAD ME WORRIED...

                    ...MORE ACTS TO GO.[∦]NO ONE ELSE TO HELP...

                    ....GET NEXT ACT READY....

                    BREAKTWO
                    ─────────

LARGE PLANK, DUMMY
MALLET
                    (ZACH STANDING BY PLANK)

*ARRANGED
AS
CATAPAULT.*
                    BACK IN TRANS...GYPSIES HAVE TEST FOR

                    LIES....BETTER THAN LIE DETECTOR...SELL

                    TICKETS...GREAT TIME...CALLED CATAPAULTING

PLACE GYPSY ON ONE END OF CAT.....

...THROW BIG ROCK ON OTHER END...

...IF HE COMES DOWN HEAD FIRST..TELLING

LIE....FEET FIRST..TRUTH......

GOOD OLD JOE YOUNG USED FOR TEST...

..THINK HE'S BEEN SNEAKING OUT W/ISOBEL..

...SEE IF IT'S TRUE....

(PICK UP JOE,PLACE ON PLANK)

JOE BOY...YOU BEEN SEEING ISOBEL???...

S.E. GROANS   NO????....TEST FOR TRUTH...DON'T HAVE

ANY BIG ROCKS HERE...LOW BUDGET....

USE MYSELF...(UP ON COFFIN)....SEE

IF HE'S LYING....(JUMP ON PLANK)

WENT UP ABOUT FIFTY FEET ...COMING DOWN..

...FEET FIRST...TRUTH...

FIFTY...FORTY...THIRTY..TWENTY..TEN...

S.E. CRASH   FIVE...(S.E.)

FELL THROUGH FLOOR....BANGED UP

PRETTY BADLY....NO SHAPE TO KISS

ISOBEL....HAVE A LITTLE PRACTICE KISS

S.E. SCREAMS   ..(OPEN COFFIN....SE.....SLAM LID)

COMMERCIAL

AFTER CATAPLT......FOLLOW UP WITH DANCE

STEP...LIVEN UP CROWD....PREFORMED

FOR CROWN PRINCE...TILL HE GOT HIS...

(SWANEE RIVER)   ...START UP BAND...

(DIRTY DANUBE)   (START DANCE...ADD LYRICS EVERY SO OFTEN)

JUNK THROWN AT ZACH
THROUGHOUT

```
S.E. HISSES...RAZZ              I'M THE ONE WHO GAVE ASTAIR LESSONS...
                                ...DON'T KNOW GOOD ACT....GREAT TALENT
                                ....PRACTICED ALL YEAR....


                      BREAK THREE
MALLET                          NEXT ON AGENDA...MIND READING ACT...
                                ....DEAR WIFE PERFECT MEDIUM...READS MY
                                MIND...LITTLE PROBLEM SOMETIMES....
                                ...(SIT IN CHAIR) READY FOR ACT...I'LL
                                THINK OF SOMETHING...(NO REACTUON)
                                MUST BE ASLEEP....BUY TWO PAT BOONE
                                ALBUMS IF ISOBEL DOES ACT....
                                (PICK UP MALLET)...GUESS WHAT DEAR????
                                ....LITTLE SUPRISE FOR DOING SUCH GREAT
S.E. SCREAMS                    ACT...(MALLET BIT)
                                GUESS SHE'S NOT IN MOOD....SOMEONE IN
                                ROOM FIGHTING HER,....BLOCKING RECEPTION..
                                ..TRY U.H.F. CHANNEL....(STILL NO REACTION)
                                ....SOMEONE IS RUINING THE ACT.....
S.E. GASPORT LAUGHING           ..GASPORT.....LOUSING UP WHOLE THING..
                                ....(MALLET BIT)
S.E. R & R MUSIC                TRY AGAIN.... OH...SOMETHING WRONG..
                                TUNED IN ON WRONG PERSON...OH NO..PAT
                                BOONE'S IN THE ACT...SHUT IT OFF.....
                                ...(PICK UP GASPORT)...DO ME LITTLE
S.E. TURNTABLE SLOWS      FAVOR...BLOCK RECEPTION......
        DOWN...THEN OFF
                                (LAFF)....GASPORT COMES THROUGH ALL TIME..
                      COMMERCIAL
GUN,STRING,MIRROR               REWORD GASPORT FOR DOING GRAND JOB...
                                ...PUT HIM IN NEXT ACT....TRICK SHOOTING..
```

                              TRICK SHOOTING MADE ME FAMOUS IN TRANS..

                                ...USE REAL BULLETTS...NO PHONEY STUFF...

                               ....NOTHING BUT BEST FOR ACT...TIE

                             GASPORT TO CEILING .. START SWINGING...

                              DO TRICK SHOTS....HIT HIM EVERY TIME..

                             ...NEVER MISS....GROANS EVERY TIME

                             BULLET HITS.....BETTER THAN GONG...

                             ...MORE VOTES.....

                                (TIE UP GASP..START SWINGING)

S.E. GROAN AFTER SHOTS   FIRST SHOT....EYES CLOSED...(SHOOT)

                               JUST GREAT....

                             NEXT...LIE ON FLOOR...(SHOOT)

                             OVER SHOULDER....

                             UNDER ARM.....

                             GRAND FINALE....RICOCHET OFF WALL...

                               ...HITS CEILING....THEN COFFIN

                             FINALLY GASPORT...WITH A MIRROR NO LESS.,..

S.E. RICO.   (PICK UP MIRROR...SHOOT)
S.E. SCREAMS   OH..I.LITTLE TROUBLE..HIT DEAR WIFE..

                             ...TRY AGAIN....

                                (REPEAT)

                               THAT'S BETTER....HIT HIM...

                             (TAKE DOWN GAS.)

                               FEEL LITTLE HEAVY...FULL OF LEAD AS

                             THEY SAY...GREAT SPIRIT THOUGH...

                             ...NEVER MISSES AN ACT...

BREAK FOUR

SNAKES, BOX W/LID

ISOBEL READY FOR NEXT ACT...DOESN'T

KNOW IT...GOING TO CHARM SAVAGE REPTILES..

..IMPORTED FROM TRANS... RAISED BY

DR. FRANK.....(PUT BOX TO EAR)

ALL IN THERE...EVERY ONE OF THEM...

GET THEM LIVENED UP..(SHAKE BOX)

...JUST FINE...HAVE TO SNEAK UP ON

HER...SUPRISE HER..(LAFF)

NEVER DID LIKE DR. FRANK...LIKES HIS SNAKE

FRIENDS EVEN LESS...SCARED STIFF OF THEM...

SOMEONE IN COFFIN
MAKE BIG RUCKUS
MOVE COFFIN AROUND

..LOADS OF FUN...(SNEAK UP ON COFFIN..

OPEN BOX & DUMP IN SNAKES)

BETTER SIT ON COFFIN...MAKE SURE

S.E. SCREAMS

THEY DON'T GET OUT.... ...SOUNDS LIKE

FUN....GREAT JOB....COULDN'T DO ANY BETTER..

...ISOBEL ALWAYS GREAT SCRAPPER...KICKED

HER OUT OF TRANS. FOR FIGHTING W/ WEREWOLVES..

..WON ALL THE TIME...NO SPORT INVOLVED...

GUESS IT'S SAFE TO GET OFF NOW....GOT

THEM UNDER CONTROL...OPEN UP...SEE HOW

SHE IS...

(SNAKES THROWN OUT AT ZACH...BIG FIGHT)

IT'S ALIVE ...IT'S ALIVE.....HELP...

...DIRTY TRICK ISOBEL....

COMMERCIAL

(ZACH ON FLOOR..SNAKE IN HAND)

                    GOT THEM UNDER CONTROL...JUST

                STARED AT THEM....(YELL) JUST

            FOR THAT ISOBEL....DO LITTLE WRESTLING MATCH...

            ..TEACH HER LESSON....USED TO BE CHAMP

            AT TRANS. UNIV....WON MEDAL. ...

                    NO HOLDS BARRED DEAR....ONE FALL...

                WINS MATCH....SHOULDER TO MAT....

                    ...(CLIMB IN)....ONE..TWO..THREE..GO..

            (START MATCH...THINGS FLY OUT OF COFFIN)

                    GOT YOU....TOO GOOD YOU YOU HUH...

            ....STOP THAT ISOBEL....CAN'T USE

                THAT HOLD...BARRED BY TRANS. ATHELETIC

            COMM......HELP...LET GO....GET ME OUT OF HERE..

            ...(RUCKUS CONT.)

            GOT YOU DEAR....BEAT YOU ALL THE TIME....

                ....(STAND UP)...WINNER & STILL CHAMP...

            ZACHERELEY...(FALL BACK INTO COFFIN)...

                ...MATCH OVER...I WON...NO MORE WRESTLING...

                .....DIRTY CHEATING GOING ON....HELP...

            ....(RUCKUS TO END)...........

S.E. FAST MUSIC
DURING MATCH

BREAK FIVE

TORCH SOAKED
W/LIGHTER FLUID

MARSHMALLOWS
PAIL OF WATER

                    NEXT ACT COMING UP...FIRE EATING...

                USUALLY DO IT MYSELF...SORE THROAT FROM

                    YELLING...DIRTY FIGHTER THAT ISOBEL...

            LEARNED IT FROM MOTHER...BAD SIDE OF TRACKS..

                    ....HAVE TO USE SOMEONE ELSE (GLANCE AT GAS?)

                YOU'RE IT....HAVE FUN....LOADS OF LAUGHS..

                ..IN TRANS...TOAST TANNA LEAVES...HERE

          USE MARSHMALLOWS....

        (PUT GASPORT ON COFFIN..PICK UP
TORCH AND LIGHT)

         OPEN WIDE....(STICK IN)....(IN W/MARSH)

S.E. LAUGHING   HE LIKES IT....GETS ALL WARM INSIDE...

         ...TOASTS THE SPIDERS HE ATE...

S.E. FIRE ENGINES   OH...SOUNDS LIKE TROUBLE...SOMEONE TURNED

         IN AN ALARM.....

      (YELL)....YOU CAN GO BACK...NO TROUBLE

         HERE...EVERYTHING UNDER CONTROL...

PAIL OF WATER ON XXX   IN THE ACT....HARMLESS FUN
    ZACH

          WISE GUYS....GO BACK PLAY CHECKERS....

        ..OR WHATEVER YOU PLAY....

          RUINED THE WHOLE ACT.....GASPORT ALL

         WET...(PULL OUT SOGGED MARSH)

           RUINED THE MARSH. TOO (THROW ON FLOOR)

         NEVER HAPPEN IN TRANS....

       COMMERCIAL

BALLOONS   BY THIS TIME FOLLIES GOING ALONG JUST
STRING

        SWELL...EVERYBODY SLEEPING....HAVE TO PULL

        STUNT TO WAKE THEM UP. ...SEND SOMEONE

        OUT OVER AUDIENCE IN BALLOON....

        DROPS MONEY DOWN....BIG FIGHT...LOTS OF

        LAFFS.....USE GASPORT AGAIN...LOVES TO

          TRAVEL....

         (TIE ON GASPORT TO BALLOONS....)

GASPORT PULLED OUT
   SLOWLY

         HE'S OFF....RIGHT OVER BALCONEY NOW...

       ...FOURTY FEET UP...OH...SOME WISE GUY

        TRYING TO BREAK BALLOONS....

S.E. BALLOONS BREAK ONE BY ONE	CUT IT OUT....ONLY ONE LEFT....
S.E. SLIDE WHISTLE	......WATCH OUT GASPORT...
	(FOLLOW DOWN WITH HEAD)
S.E. CRASH	RIGHT ON TOP OF JOE YOUNG...
S.E. MOB UP & OUT	..SHAKEN UP... ALL GRABBING THE MONEY...

OH..PRESS BOYS ARE LEAVING...HAVE TO

MAKE DEADLINE....HOPE THEY GIVE XXX

FOLLIES GOOD RIGHT UP....

.... PAYED ENOUGH..(LAFF)....

BREAK SIX

WIRES
FLASHPOT

(GASPORT ON COFFIN)

HE GOT SHAKEN UP THERE....NOT HURT THOUGH...

...NEED HIM FOR NEXT ACT...REALLY GIVE HIM

JOLT...WIRE HIM UP...TWO THOUSAND

VOLTS....THIS ACTX DATES BACK TO

DR. FRANK....TIME HE BUILT FRANKIE...

...DONE EVERY YEAR AS MONUMENT TO HIM...

...CALLED CHARGING UP THE BRAIN.....COMMONLY

KNOWN AS ELECTROCUTION.....

(HOOK UP WIRES)... TAKE SOME PEASANT...

(PAT GASPORT)....CONNECT HIM TO JUICE...

...TURN ON....EVERYBODY SITS AROUND...

...WAIT TILL HE COOKS....IF HE PULLS

THROUGH...EVERYBODY THROWS MONEY....PEASANT

TAKES IT AND BUYS WHATEVER HE WANTS...

DID IT LAST YEAR......RAN UP

QUITE A BILL....TOCK TWO WEEKS BEFORE

YOU COULD TOUCH HIM...ALL CHARGED UP...

FLASHPOT IN GASPORT

...KISSED ISOBEL AND CURLED HER HAIR...

..PAY MONEY AT THE BEAUTY PARLOR...

GET IT HERE FREE......READY TO

S.E. ELECTRICAL NOISES

THROW SWITCH..(THROW)

JUST GRAND.....WORKING OUT SWELL...

LIGHTS DIM

GASPORT USING TO MUCH,....OVERLOADING

CIRCUIT......(LOCK WORRIED).....

...DOESN'T LOOK TOO GOOD...(YELL)

STOP USING SO MUCH GASPORT....

FLASHPOT OFF

YOU DID IT THIS TIME....BLEW A FUSE....

LIGHTS UP

SATISFIED ????......

COMMERCIAL

CANNON
FLASHPOT

LAST TRICK OF FOLLIES....GREATEST OF

ALL...THE SHOOT OFF...SIGNALS END OF

FOLLIES.....SHOOT HIM RIGHT OUT OF

CRYPT....PARACHUTE OPENS OVER TIMES SQ...

....BIG DOINGS.....

MAKE LITTLE SPEACH BEFORE SHOOT OFF

BEEN GRAND SHOW...DEAR WIFE BIG HELP..

S.E. RAZZ

GASPORT TOO.....I WAS THE BEST THOUGH ....

WISE GUYS.....HOPE WE CAN DO ANOTHER FOLLIES..

...(PULL ROPE)

FLASHPOT OFE

AND THAT IS THE END OF THE FOLLIES 1960...

...OH..LITTLE TROUBLE UP THERE...PARACHUTE

NOT OPENING.....WELL...TOUGH LUCK FOR HIM...

                              I'LL DO A LITTLE SONG BEFORE

S.E. MOB   YOU LEAVE....WROTE IT MYSELF...

                  OH....COME BACK. ..HAVE TO COLLECT MONEY

                  FOR NEXT YEARS SHOW....DON'T LEAVE...WE

                          DON'T HAVE ANY MONEY ...ENNIS HAS IT

                  ALL...WON'T GIVE ANY AWAY....

                      DON'T GO

          BREAK SEVEN CLOSE

                              JUST WAITING FOR NEWSPAPERS....READ

                      GRAND RIGHTUPS....

S.E. CAR STOPPING

    PAPERS THROWN ON STAGE   HERE THEY ARE...READ THE REPORTS..

                  (OPEN FIRST PAPER)

                              NEW YORK TONIGH WITNESSED ZACH.
                              AND COMPANY PREFORMING THE TRANS.
                              FOLLIES. IT WAS TRULY THE WORST
                              MESS WE HAVE EVER SEEN. THE ACTS
                              WERE GRUESOME(THROW DOWN)

                          DOESN'T KNOW WHAT HE'S TALKING ABOUT

                  (NEXT PAPER)

                              ZACHERELY TONIGHT CAME FORTH WITH HIS
                              USUAL SHOWMANSHIP (SMILE) AND PRESENTED
                              TRANS. FOLLIES. ALL THIS WRITER CAN
                              SAY IS...TAKE IT BACK TO TRANS.

                      BUNCH OF NUTS IN THAT BUSINESS...

                  ...GUESS I WON THE CONTEST THOUGH...GET TO KISS

                  DEAR WIFE...GASPORT RUNNER UP...HE GETS

                      FILM....(CLIMB IN COFFIN)

                      PUCKER UP DEAR (PUCKER UP LIPS)

                  (BIG FIGHT TO END)

S.E. THEME   (ZACH ON LADDER PUTTING UP DECORATIONS)

                    GREAT NEWS....JUST RECIEVED TELEGRAM

                    FROM PRIME MINISTER OF TRANS....HE'S ARRIVING

                    HERE TONIGHT FOR A TWO WEEK VISIT....SUMMIT

                    TALKS WITH ALL THE BOYS....(DOWN FROM LADDER)

                    HAVE TO GET THINGS READY FOR MEETING....ALL

                    THE BIG BOYS WILL BE HERE....KRUSCH....*IKE*.....

                    deGAULLE....AND THE PRIME MINISTER OF TRANS...

                    ....(NAIL CREPE PAPER ON COFFIN) EVERYBODY

S.E. ISOBEL   HAS TO LOOK NICE MY DEAR... BIG DOINGS YOU

                    KNOW.....EVEN GASPORT HAS TO LOOK HIS BEST...

                    ... I'M REALLY THE ONE THEY WANT TO SEE

                    YOU KNOW....THE REST OF THEM ARE HERE FOR THE

                    RIDE....I'M THE ONE WHO RUNS TRANSYLVANIA....THAT

                    JERK THEY HAVE IN OFFICE NOW CAN'T EVEN SPELL

                    OWN NAME.....LOTS TO DO...HAVE TO MAKE UP

                    THE FAVORS , PLAN THE ENTERTAINMENT, SHARPEN

                    THE PENCILS AND EVEYTHING....(PICK UP MALLET)

                    JUST IN CASE WE HAVE ANY SHOW OFFS.....LIKE EBERLE..

                    ...HE'S GOT ANOTHER BLOB TONIGHT....O.K. EB...

                    ...LET'S START THAT THING... (FILM DOESN'T START)

                    (YELLING) EBERLE.....(GROWING MADDER) EBERLE..

                    ....YARNUSH...GO IN AND WAKE HIM UP........

BREAK ONE

TABLE, CHAIRS
                    (ARRANGE CHAIRS)

                    HAVING A LITTLE PROBLEM HERE WITH SEATING

                    ARRANGEMENTS.....HAVE TO KEEP PRIME MIN. AWAY

                    FROM ISOBEL....MAY SNEAK OVER AND START SMOOCHING

```
S.E.  LOUD KISSING                (GLANCE AT COFFIN..S.E. CONTINUES)

                                  PRACTICING MY DEAR ????...(PICK UP

                                  MALLET ..WALK TO COFFIN) I'VE GOT SOMETHING

S.E. SCREAMS                      FOR YOU MY DEAR(MALLET BIT) ...THAT TAKES

LIGHTS FLICKER THEN OUT           CARE OF YOU DEAR...(LAFF)....  OH...WHAT

                                  GOING ON HERE...(IN DARKNESS) JUST A MINUTE

                                  ...LITTLE TROUBLE HERE...(LIGHT CANDLES)

                                  GASPORT...HAVE YOU BEEN FOOLING WITH THE JUICE

S.E HIC CUPS          BOY?   (YELL) NOT THAT JUICE ...THE POWER....

                      ....I'LL JUST CALL CON EDISON...MUST BE THEIR

                      FAULT..(PICK UP PHONE)  GET CON EDISON DEAR...

                      .......HELLO....THIS IS ZACH..WHAT'S GOING ON

                      DOWN HERE...NO LIGHTS..THAT'S WHAT.....WHAT DO YOU

                      MEAN I DIDN'T PAY MY BILL ...I SENT GASPORT

                      OVER LAST WEEK....OF COURSE I'M SURE...OH

                      WAIT JUST A MINUTE HERE.....(PUT DOWN PHONE...

S.E. LAUGHING         WALK OVER AND PICK UP GASPORT)

                      GASPORT..YOU DID IT THIS TIME BOY...(MALLET BIT)

                              COMMERCIAL


                      LAST TIME I'LL GIVE THAT GASPORT ANY MONEY...

                      ...HE WENT OUT AND BOUGHT SPIDERS....(PICK UP PHONE)

                      LOOK, THERE'S GOING TO BE A BIG MEETING HERE...

                      MY CREDITS GOOD .........PUT KOCH ON .......KOCH???..

                      .....LOOK, I'M A LITTLE SHORT ON MONEY NOW....HOW ABOUT

                      SOME JUICE ON THE CUFF......GOOD BOY....I'LL TAKE CARE

LIGHTS FLICKER    OF YOU...... GREAT,BOY.... (HANG UP)....
THEN ON
                      WELL , THAT PROBLEMS TAKEN CARE OF....(LAFF)

                      EVERYTHING UNDER CONTROL....

S.E. BOMBS...TRACTORS        (YELL) NOW WHAT????....WHAT'S GOING ON UP
```

THERE????? (DIRT FALLS ON ZACH)

(PICK UP PHONE) GIVE ME MOSES...HURRY UP....

.........THAT YOU MOSES?....WHAT ARE YOU DOING...

......(ANGRILY) TEARING DOWN MY CRYPT TO BUILD A

SLUM?????..... WE'LL JUST SEE ABOUT THAT.....

NOBOBY'S GOING TO BUILD A SLUM IN MY CRYPT ..

(SLAM DOWN REVIEVER) THIS MEANS WAR......

CANNON, GUNS   ... WHAT MORE CAN HAPPEN????? (BRING IN CANNON)
FLASHPOT IN
   CANNON   THIS'LL GIVE THEM A JOLT (LAFF) (CANNON OFF)

GOT THEM. (LAFF) ....THERE'S THE WHITE FLAG....

(YELLING) O.K. ALL OF YOU GET OUT OF HERE....

....AND DON'T COME BACK IF YOU KNOW WHAT'S GOOD FOR

S.E. DISORDERLY   YOU.... OH...HERE COMES THE PRESS....COME ON IN
   MOB
 UP & OUT   BOYS..... TAKE YOUR SEATS.....I'D LIKE TO MAKE

A LITTLE STATEMENT BEFORE THE BOYS GET HERE.....

S.E. HISSES..BOOS   .....WELL..IF THAT'S THE WAY YOU FEEL (SIT

IN CHAIR....LOK HURT) EVERYBODY'S AGAINST ME...

BREAK TWO

SPIDERS, FLOUR,   (ZACH AT COFFIN)
WATER, TRAYS
SNAKES, FRANK. BUNS   GETTING THE REFRESHMENTS READY HERE....
EGGS
               ...MOTHER ZACH'S RECIPE....JUST THE THING

FOR SUMMIT TAIKS.....KEEPS EVERYBODY MAD...

MORE FUN THAT WAY... (PICK UP SPIDER)

THE WAY TO DO IT OF COURSE,IS TO DIP THEM

IN TANNA JUICE MIXED WITH GROUND BONES....

THE BEST PART THOUGH IS THE GOOSE EGG...LENDS

THAT LITTLE TANG.... (BREAK OPEN EGG..DUMP

IN FLOUR..ADD WATER) JUST GREAT....THEY'LL

LOVE IT......

```
                                (PUT GOOK ON BUNS)  NOW WE JUST ADD

                                THE SPIDER TO THE BUNS...AND THE MOST

                                NOURISHING PART..THE SNAKES.....CHOPPED

                                UP FINLY.....(ADD SPIDERS AND SNAKES)

S.E. MOB                        AND HERE WE...(CUT OFF BY NOISE)  NOW WHAT???

                                ...OH NO...THERE HAVING ANOTHER PARTY UPSTAIRS

S.E. LOUD MUSIC                 ...... WE CAN'T HAVE THIS DURING THE MEETING .

    CONTINUES                   .... EVERYTHINGS GOING WRONG TODAY.... WHERE'S

                                THE FUSE BOX FOR UPSTAIRS.....(WAIK TO WALL)

METAL BOX ON WALL               HERE WE ARE.....THIS'LL STOP THEM (TURN FUSE)

S.E. TURNTABLE SLOWS            (LAFF)  THERE.... THAT'S THAT......THAT
DOWN
                                MUSIC WAS KILLING ME.....

S.E.  PEOPLE STAMPING           OH NO....(PLASTER FALLS FROM CEILING)
ON FLOOR
                                (YELL) ALRIGHT ...HAVE YOUR PARTY...I HOPE

                                YOU GO DEAF...(TURN FUSE)

S.E. TURNTABLE SPEEDS           (ZACH SITS IN CHAIR...HOLDS GASPORT IN
UP AGAIN                              LAP)

                                GASPORT....YOU STILL LOVE ME DON'T YOU?????

S.E. LAUGHING                   WELL DON'T YOU????? (PUT GASPORT ON COFFIN)

                        (WEAKLY)ISOBEL?...DEAR?.....SWEETUM?....SHE'S STILL

                                OUT COLD...(STARE AT CAMERA WITH HEAD IN HAND)


                        COMMERCIAL

SE.MUSIC STILL                  (STILL IN CHAIR)
PLAYING
                                NO USE.... (YELL) YOU BOYS UP THERE...PUT

                                DOWN THE DICE AND LISTEN TO ME....YOU'D BETTER

                                GET OUT...LOOKS LIKE THEXX WHOLE THINGS OFF..

S.E. MOB _UP&OUT                ....WELL.... MIGHT AS WELL EAT THE REFRESHMENTS

                                ....(PICK UP EMPTY BUN)  UM...DELICIOUS....

                                .....(PUT DOWN) JUST NOT HUNGRY....ALL MY PLANS
```

175

	RUINED......MIGHT AS WELL GO UPSTAIRS AND
	JOIN THE PARTY...(YELL) I'LL BE RIGHT UP
MUSIC STOPS S.E. MOB	BOYS... OH..~~S~~ THEY'RE LEAVING......WELL
	IF THEY DON'T WANT ME ...I'LL JUST STAY
STRING TO GASPORT PULL OFF CAMERA	HERE AND HAVE A LITTLE FUN WITH GASPORT
	....GASPORT...COME BACK HERE....EVEN GASPORT
	DOESN'T WANT ME...I'M JUST AN OUTCAST....
	....(SIT IN CHAIR AND DO NOTHING FOR ABOUT
S.E. SOMETHING KNOCKED OVER	FIFTEEN SECONDS) WHO'S THERE........WHO IS IT....
	(JUMP UP) (YELL) KENNEDY...GET OUT OF
	HERE.....THAT'S A BOMB YOU'VE GOT THERE BOY...
FLASH POT SET BY COFFIN	...BE CAREFUL WITH THAT THING...(DUCK BEHIND COFFIN)
	I WAS ONLY KIDDING YOU.....X YOU'RE DOING
	A GREAT BANG UP JOB WITH THE BOYS......
FLASH POT OFF	(GROANS....COFFS....TO MOVIE)
PROPS:	BREAK THREE
HAT AND CANE	(ZACH ON FLOOR....GROANING)
	OH ...THAT KENNEDY...HE ALMOST KILLED ME....
	....(YELL)YARNUSH..LOCK THE DOOR...KEEP THEM
	OUT BOY.... (DRAG YOURSELF TO CHAIR)
	(SPOT HAT AND CANE) OH...(PICK UP) MIGHT AS
	WELL PRACTICE THE ENTERTAINMENT.....
	....LITTLE DANCE NUMBER....RAGE BACK IN TRANS...
MUSIC) THAT OLD SOFT SHOE	.... (PUT ON HAT ...START DANCE)
	GIVE ME THAT OLD SOFT SHOE XXXX I SAID THAT OLD SOFT SHOE A ONE, A TWO, A DOODALEE DOODALEE DOO GIVE ME THAT OLD SOFT SHOE AND NOTHING ELSE WILL DO..(CUT OFF)
S.E. GASPORT LAUGHING..RAZZ	(THROW DOWN HAT AND CANE)

```
                        GASPORT...I KNOW YOU IN HERE....(WAIK TO

                        SULFUR PIT)  I SEE YOU GASPORT....(LOSE

S.E.  SPLASHING           BALANCE...FALL IN)


                          GOT YOU GASPORT.....I'LL FIX YOU BOY..
        CAMERA STILL IN
        CRYPT AREA        ....COME ON....OH ...SOMEBODY TOOK

                        THE LADDER.....(YELL) HELP.....EBERLE...

                        ...HELP ME....GET ME OUT OF HERE.....

                        ..YARNUSH.....ISOBEL......HELP.....


                        COMMERCIAL


                        (ZACH..WET AND GASPORT IN HAND...CRAWL

                        BACK TO CRYPT)  SOME HELP YOU WERE GASPORT...

S.E. LAUGHING           .....  I DON'T KNOW WHAT I'M GOING TO DO W/YOU
                                                          MY
S.E. ISOBEL             BOY.....YOU'RE GETTING JUST LIKE XXX SON....

S.E. " CRYING           HE'S YOUR SON TOO YOU KNOW....  I KNOW DEAR...

                        ....(OPEN UP COFFIN)  NOW NOW...HAVE A SPIDER

S.E. SLURPIG            DEAR...(DROP ONE IN) .... THERE YOU ARE ...THAT'S

                        BETTER.........WONDER WHERE THE BOYS ARE....

S.E. PHONE             ...THEYR'E A LITTLE LATE....... THAT MUST BE

                        THEM NOW....(PICK UP PHONE)  HELLO....OH

                        HELLO NIKKY....HOW'S EVERYTHING AT THE KREMLIN...

                     ....XXXX  HEAR YOU'RE A LITTLE SHORT OF VODKA....

                        PLENTY HERE YOU KNOW....WHAT....WHAT DO YOU MEAN

                        YOU'RE NOT COMING....OH...LITTLE UNDER THE WEATHER..

                        .....TRY A RAW GOOSE EGG....FIX YOU UP IN NO TIME..

                        ....WE DON'T NEED YOU HERE ANYWAY... THE REST OF

                     US WILL HANDLE EVERYTHING....OH...ALL THE BOYS WILL

                        BE HERE....GREAT FUN....TOO BAD YOU CAN'T COME...

                        (HANG UP)  (LAFF) THAT'S MORE SPIDERS FOR ME....
```

                              DON'T NEED HIM ANYWAY....HE JUST GETS

IN THE WAY....

          BACK IN TRANSYLVANIA....EVERYTIME

WE HAVE SUMMIT TAIK....THERE'S A BIG

CEREMONY BEFORE TAIKS START....THROWING A

PEASANT TO THE WEREWOLVES....SOUGHT OF GETS THE

MEETING OFF ON THE RIGHT FOOT...HERE IN U.S.A.

WE CAN'T USE WEXREWOLVES....XXX BOARD OF

HEALTH WON'T ALLOW IT...TOO MESSY....

          WE USE A DIFFERENT METHOD...CALIED SHISHKABOB-

ING....TAKE A PEASANT (GRAB GASPORT) AND PUT

HIM ON A TABLE.....EVERYBODY GRABS A SWORD AND

S.E. GASPORT   STICKS THE PEASANT WITH IT ...DON'T WORRY

BOY....WON'T FEEL A THING......THE THINGS IS...

IF THE PEASANT PULLS THROUGH....THE MEETING'S A

SUCCESS.......BETTER TEST GASPPRT...DON'T WANT

HIM TO KICK OFF ON ME..(LAFF)....(GRAB SWORD..

S.E. MOANS   STICK GASPORT) TAKE IT EASY BOY....

          THERE WE ARE...NOW WE PULL OUT THE SWORDS AND

SEE IF HE RECOVERED.........GASPORT??? (FRANTICLY)

GASPORT????? (LOOK WORRIED) GASPORT OLD BOY

S.E. LAUGHING   SPEAK TO ME...   GOOD BOY....HAD ME WORRIED THERE

..... BETTER TRY IT WITH ISOBEL....I THINK

SHE'D WORK A LITTLE BETTER....(INTO COFFIN.....

S.E. ISOBEL   ....BIG RUCKUS) EASY DEAR....ALL IN THE NAME OF
SCREAMING

GLORIOUS SCIENCE........

BREAK FOUR

S.E. MOANS   DEAR???? (PULL OUT SWORDS) HERE WE GO

S.E. SCREAMS

SEE MY DEAR...YOU'RE O.K.   ....OH

SHE LIKES IT....WELL MY DEAR...I'LL

JUST PUT THEM BACK IN....FUN ISN'T IT

DEAR.... PRIME MINISTER SHOULD BE GETTING

HERE SOON.....START THE MEETING WHEN HE

S.E. PARADE MARCHING   GETS HERE
MUSIC
                     OH HERE HE COMES...TICKER TAPE PARADE
SIRENS...GUNSHOTS
                 UP BROADWAY.....GREAT WELCOME.....

                 OH XXXXX....NO....NOT....(YELLING) IT'S

                 KENNEDY...WHAT'S HE DOING NOW...(RUN OFF CAMERA)

CAMERA STAYS IN
CRYPT AREA   (ZACH WALKS IN...SITS IN CHAIR SLOUCHING)

                 (FURIOUSLY) HE'S DONE IT AGAIN ....

                 HE LOCKED UP THE PRIME MINISTER......

                 THAT BOYS A LOAD OF LAFFS.....

                 THE PRIME MINISTER IN JAIL...THAT'S

                 NO WAY TO TREAT A DIGNITARY.....HERE FOR

                 IMPORTANT TALKS....HE CAN'T GET AWAY W/ THIS

                 .....I'LL SETTLE THIS NOW...(PICK UP PHONE)

                 GET ME KENNEDY.......

                 LOOK HERE KENNEDY....WHAT'S THE WRAP...

                 ..LITTERING THE SIDEWALK????....HE DIDN'T THROW

                 THAT STUFF....THEY THREW IT AT HIM.....YOU'RE

                 GOING TO THROW THE WHAT AT HIM??????.....

                 KENNEDY I'M WARNING YOU FOR THE LAST TIME...

                 ..LAY OFF MY BOYS.....

            COMMERCIAL

                 WELL ...WE STILL HAVE IKE, MACMILLAN

                 AND DEGAULLE.....MEETING'S STILL ON....I'LL

                 TAKE OVER FOR THE PRIME MINISTER...DON'T NEED HI

S.E. PHONE   ANYWAY....

                    HELLO....MACMILLAN HUH..PUT HIM ON

                 ....HELLO MAC? ZACH MAC....WEDDING....

              OH YEAH.....FLOWER BOY???....OH....GUESS

           YOU CAN'T MAKE IT THEN.....WELL ...THAT'S TOO

        BAD...HAD A BIG THING ALL SET UP....FOOD

    SOME BOOZE...GREAT FUN....CAN'T YOU POSTPONE

    THE WEDDING....OH I SEE.....WELL....WE'LL

        JUST HAVE TO GET ALONG W/OUT YOU BOY....SORRY

  THAT'S THE WAY IT GOES,....NO HE'S NOT HERE YET

  HAD A LITTLE ,UH, TOUBLE WITH SOME OF THE BOYS....

       ....LITTLE TIED UP(LAFF)....I'M TAKING HIS

         PLACE....WHY DIDN'T I GET INVITED TO THE WEDDING.L.

       ...WHO DO YOU THINK TAUGHT THAT GUY HOW TO TAKE

        PICTURES....ME THAT'S WHO....WELL I'VE

    GOT WORK TO TO....MEETING'S SET FOR ANY MINUTE

    NOW.....SO LONG MAC...(HANG UP)

        WELL, AT LEAST IKE AND DEGAULLE WILL BE

        HERE....

     HAVE A WEDDING ANY DAY...CAN'T HAVE BIG

     SUMMIT TALKS THOUGH....HE'LL BE SORRY.....

     ...

BREAK FIVE

                    HIGH POINT OF EVENING IS THE GRAND OLD
BOWL, CUPS
                 TOASTING CEREMONY....EVERYBODY LIKES THAT PART(LAFF)

         HAVE THE BREW AS THEY SAY, ALL MIXED UP....

      ONE PART TANNA JUICE..ONE PART LEMON JUICE AND TEN

         PARTS JUST PLAIN JUICE(LAFF) HAVE TO TEST IT

MAKE SURE IT'S ALL RIGHT....(TAKE CUP

AND FILL) LITTLE PRACTICE TOAST ....

TO BOB KENNEDY....MAY HE GET CAUGHT IN ONE

OF HIS OWN SPEED TRAPS (LAFF)

HUM...LITTLE TOO MUCH TANNA....ADD SOME

MORE BOOZE (POUR IN) TAKE ANOTHER TASTE....

..(DRINK 2ND CUP) MORE LEMON JUICE (ADD)

(TASTE AGAIN) MORE TANNA (GETTING WOOZZY)

MORE LEMON (ADD) TASTE AGAIN HERE (TASTE)

MORE BOOZE (COMPLETELY DRUNK NOW)

MORE LEMON....... WHERE'S THE LEMON.....

..(STAGGER AROUND) GASPORT ...YOU HIDING

THE LEMONS BOY???......ISOBEL....WHERE'S THE

S.E. ISOBEL   LEMON DEAR....HAS TO HAVE IT YOU KNOW.....

YOU WANT SOME DEAR.....(FILL CUP) HERE WE

GO (POUR IN) STOP MOVING...OH ...JUST

A MINUTE...THERE ARE TWO OF YOU....STOP THAT

DEAR ....OH....GETTING LITTLE SICK HERE....

...(PASS OUT)

COMMERCIAL

PAIL OF WATER   FEEL LITTLE FUNNY HERE....YARNUSH BOY...

...GET ME A GLASS OF WATER..... (WATER ON ZACH)

NOT THAT WAY BOY....MUST HAVE PASSED OUT THERE ..

.... BE ALL RIGHT IN A MINUTE...TAKE ANOTHER

SHOT...THAT'LL FIX ME UP FINE....(DRINK)

O.K. NOW..... (UP OFF FLOOR) AFTER WE ALL

GET GOT UP AFTER THE TOASTING (LAFF) WE GO BACK TO

THE DISCUSSION......IF THINGS DON'T GO RIGHT...

....WE HAVE A LITTLE GAME WE PLAY...REAL FUN TYPE

OF THING....IF TWO PEOPLE HAVE A LITTLE
ARGUMENT...PLAY TUG OF WAR WITH MONSTER...
....(PICK UP MONSTER(?))   ONE PERSON
TAKES ONE END AND THE OTHER TAKE THE OTHER END..
.... PULL UNTILL MONSTER COMES APART....THE ONE
WITH THE BIG END WINS....TEST OUT JOE YOUNG HERE..
.... (PUT ONE END IN COFFIN ....DUMMY ~~~~~ LOOS
IN CHEST AREA SO AS TO FALL APART AT LITTLE
PULL)
SAY I'M HAVING A LITTLE ARGUMENT W/ISOBEL...
...O.K. DEAR START PULLING....(PULL)....OH...
SEE NOW I HAVE THE MOST OF IT...SO I WIN THE ARG-

S.E. ISOBEL SCREAMING UMENT......ALLRIGHT DEAR.....(SWITCH PIECES)
YOU WON......HAVE TO BE CAREFUL NOT TO
HURT HER FEELINGS,.....OF COURSE IT'S MORE FUN
WHEN THREE OR FOUR HAVE ARGUMENT....GREAT
SPORT INVOLVED....MONSTER ALWAYS LOSES....

BREAK SIX

THEY'RE SURE TAKING THEIR TIME GETTING HERE..
...MAYBE KENNEDY ....NO HE WOULDN'T DARE....
...NOT IKE...NO....

S.E. PHONE   HELLO.. .OH IT'S YOU IKE....WHERE ARE
YOU...GOLF COURSE.....OH NO....GOLF DATE...
...WITH WHO...OH.....I SEE....WHAT ABOUT DICK??
...CADDYING....OH...WELL.....TOO BAD....
HAVE TO GET ALONG WITHOUT YOU THEN....ALL THIS
FOOD....GOV'T SUBSIDY...NO IT'S NOT THAT MUCH

COULD YOU DO ME A FAVOR?...I WANT TO

GET RID OF KENNEDY....NO, NOT THAT ONE...

...███ KENNEDY OF N.Y......GIVING ME

TROUBLE.....INVESTIGATIONX??..THAT'LL DO

JUST FINE....O.K. SO LO NG IKE..(HANG UP)

WELL...THAT LEAVES DEGAULLE AND ME...NOT MUCH

OF A MEETING.... HOW COULD THEY ALL IGNORE

SUCH AN IMPORTANT MEETING?....FUTURE OF WORLD

AT STAKE.....

AT END OF MEETING....EVERYBODY TIRED....

...SIT IN A CIRCLE LIKE SO(PUT GASPORT ON FLOOR

AND SIT NEXT TO HIM) EVERYBODY TELLS STORY...

.....LAFF IT UP A LITTLE....NOW I ALWAYS TELL

THE ONE ABOUT THE LITTLE OLD MUMMY WHO

WAS CROSSING THE NILE WHEN ALL OF A SUDDEN

SHE FALLS IN...A LITTLE WEREWOLF COMES UP TO

HER AND WHAT DO YOU THINK HE SAYS......

S.E. GASPORT   HE SAYS..... (GASPORT LAUGHS) GASPORT...
LAUGHING

I DIDN'T FINISH IT YET BOY....

AFTER WE TELL THE STORIES WE SIT AND WATCH ONE

MINUTE HOME MOVIES....WE HAVE K'S HERE TONIGHT..

COMMERCIAL

S.E. PHONE   AFTER WE SEE THE MOVIES (CUT OFF)

THAT COULD ONLY BE ONE PERSON....

(PICK UP PHONE). ..HELLO ...I KNOW...

IT'S DEGAULLE...PUT HIM ON.....HELLO

D GAULLE....WHY CAN'T YOU MAKE IT...OH...

..LITTLE TROUBLE W/THE PEASANTS HUH??¢?TOO BAD

WELL...YOU KNOW HOW I'D HANDLE THEM DON'T

YOU....THAT'S THE WAY BOY....(LAFF)

TOO MESSY HUH????....THEY WHAT......

...OH...I SEE...NO WONDER YOU'RE MAD...

...ROBBING GRAVES.....(COVER UP RECIEVER)

GREAT BUNCH OF BOYS OVER THERE...(UNCOVER)

YES...I KNOW...IT'S JUST TERRIBLE....

.... WELL HAVE FUN .....MEETING...WHAT MEETING??

...THE WHOLE THING'S OFF....(SLAM DOWN REC.)

WORKED SO HARD.....PLANS ALL RUINED...

....PRIME MINISTER IN JAILX......

KENNEDY OUT GUNNING FOR ME...ALMOST GOT KILLED

FOR WHAT...???? ....NOBODY'S EVEN COMING..

.. LITTLE THEY CARE....WELL I STILL HAVE

S.E. MOANS   GASPORT..... I KNOW BOY....TOUGH LUCK....

....WELL...HAVE TO FINISH UP THE REFRESHMENTS

BY MYSELF....(START EATING....THEN THROW DOWN)

(ON VERGE OF TEARS) NOBODY CARES ABOUT ME...

.....HAD ALL THE PLANS MADE....MONSTER PULLING...

...SHISHKABOBBING....TOASTING CEREMONY ....

....STORY TELLING.....I WON'T EVEN GET A CHANCE

S.E. RAZZ   TO TELL MY GREAT STORY... EBERLE???? I SUPPOSE

YOU HAVE A BETTER ONE....OH NO...NOT THE BLOB...

.. GET ME OUT OF HERE...(TO MOVIE)

BREAK SEVEN (CLOSE)

(SITTING ON FLOOR BY COFFIN) NOTHING TO

DO .....MIGHT AS WELL PLAY CARDS W/ISOBEL...

...EVEN THOUGH SHE CHEATS ...SOMETHING TO DO....

```
S.E.   PARTY MUSIC....LOU D            THERE GOES THE PARTY AGAIN....

          CONTINUES             ...CAN'T EVEN HAVE   PEACE  AND QUIET...

                                  ......
S.E.  BLASTING..TRACTORS           (DIRT..PLASTER FALLS ON ZACH)
      CONT. ALSO
                                    IT'S MOSES AGAIN....(YELL) GET OUT OF
                                HERE
S.E. SIRENS...GUNSHOTS..           (FLASHPOT SET BY COFFIN..OFF)

MOB YELLING   .SCREAMS          (COFFING)   NOW KENNEDY.....

                                (JUNK KEEPS FALLING ON ZACH)....HELP...

                                ...GET ME OUT OF HERE.........

S.E. GASPORT LAUGHING
                                ....ALLRIGHT...ALL OF YOU ...JUST GO AWAY.

                                .....   SHUT UP GASPORT....

S.E. CONTINUE
   TO END                       HELP........GET ME CUT OF HERE....

                                GET OUT....LEAVE ME ALONE....

                                .......


                                   END........
```

PROP LIST   TUESADY   ZACK SHOW TAPED AFTERNOON

12 ROLLS CREPE STREAMSERS

FOUR PACKAGES 1/4 " STREAMERS

TEN PACKAGES OF CONFETTI
LARGE WATERMELON

  BANANAS

LARGE CAN TOMATO JUICE

 FOUR PARTY HATS
     TWO STIFF TWO CREPE PAPER IF POSSIBLE

ENGLISH BOBBY'S HAT

    7 3/8 (GO TO BROOKS!)

OFF WHITE HOSP ORDERLY JACKET   SIZE 40

OFF WHITE AMBULANCE DRIVER HAT SIZE 7 3/8

(FLASH POWDER ENOUGH FOR ONE GOOD BLAST)

TRAY OF JELLO FROM LORRIES

CHEEZE CLOTH PKGE (ON HAND I THINK)

BURLAP BLKT
DARK OLD DRAEPE

 SMALL RUBBERHOSE

KNIFE

SPIDER

CLEAN BEAKERS
PITCHER
CARDIFF

RUB TREE

TWO FEMALE DUMS
    DUMMIES
  (ONE IS J OE

IN SKIRTS

CANNON
FLASH PWDER
WHISTLE
RERER

TRAY OF JELL

TAPE TO HOLD
  JOE ON
  SWING

OVERHEAD MIKE   ROPE FOR GASPT
     RIFLE AND FLOUR

RIG TRAPEZE

Film to Empire.
Cue card for YES.
Call Pete about weekend?
   Tues. Party.
streight Jacket. —
give last inserts to Barney
cue card (close speech.
mirror.

Portman
Rinnke
Uftro - dus
  Martin Poy
Projidon

DISC·O·TEEN SCRIPTS

DISC·O·TEEN RAN MONDAY THROUGH FRIDAY LIVE AT 6 P.M. A FEW HOURS LATER EACH FRIDAY NIGHT, AN ADDITIONAL EPISODE WAS TAPED FOR SATURDAY 5 P.M. BROADCAST. ON THE FOLLOWING PAGES ARE TWO *DISC·O·TEEN* SCRIPTS.

(1) DISCO TEEN   FRIDAY   FEB 25   6 Pm   one

                                                    PROPS   DUCK?

                                                    ELECTRIC MACHINE

                        (AC LINE IN CAve)

ECU   SPARK MACHINE   SPARK   CUE

                          TC
                          ET   "I SEE THE LIGHT" 2 10

                              BACK TO THE SPARK EACH TIME THE MUSIC FAD

                                        FADES

                          ET " 634-5789" 2 55
              SEGTC ET "

         PREVIEW PROMO SAT SHOW   "THE LEFT BAND" MUSIC
                                          RCA

                              5 PM   GOG O CONTEST
                                    BIG NOTHING PRIZE

                              THE TOUGHEST SHOW ON TV

         SEG ET "I FOUGHT THE LAW" 2 07

CAV E   INTERVIEW THE GUESTS   OR THE BAND GROUP MUSICIANS

                          MAYBE MAKE IT BIG LIKE THE MAMAS AND POPA
                                                    POPAS

         (HOLD ON INTERVIEW TILL BEAT PICKS UP)

         CUE "ET "CALIFORNIA DREAMING " 2 37

              SEG TC " GOOD LOVIN" 2 28

COMMERCIAL

         GUEST CUTE TO INTRO THE NEXT SET: ET "STOP" 2 05

6:16   SEGTC " THE CHEATER" 2 38

                                            SOUNDS OF SILENCE"
                                   SEG   ET " 22 443 MICHELLE"

6:24 ↓

FR FEB 25 6 PM TWO

the shepherds

THE AMATEUR BAND FROM GRIGGSTOWN NJ

1

2

3

6 33

COMMERCIAL LEAd in by the zak

~~MMMMMMMMMMMM~~

AN ANCIENT OLDEE :

~~MMMMMMXMMMXMMMMMM~~

"MEMPHIS " 2 28

ET ~~"THIS GOLDEN RING" 2 15~~

SEG TC "WAIT" 2 13

SEG ET "INSIDE LOOKING OUT" 2 58

CREDITS SSS

ONE
AT BANDSTAND

PROPS   PRIZE IN BAG?
ALL GUESTS CLOTHES IN FLOOR   :   DANCER CONTEST
MAIN ENTRANCE DOORS OPEN FOR AIR   NUMBERS
                                           AND PIES
FIRE ESCAPE DOOR " "   THE WISHING WELL

JOHN THE COP KEEP ALL BACK FROM DOOR AREA

set up the OPENING CREDIT ON LGE BLACK AEREA:

- - - - - - - - - - - - - - - - - - - - - - - - - -

GROUP SHOT   ET   "NITE TIME"   2 29

                  SEG TC   "JUST LIKE ME" 2 23

SUPER LOWER CORNER TITLE CARD

TOP OF LADDER SHOT IN CAVE   ZACK GREET THE MOB....

                                        THE LEFT BANKERS

                                        WM BONNIE

                                        THE DEAR WIFE IN THE BOX

                " A MOMENT OF SILENT REVERENCE FOR THE

                  PROGRAMS YOU SWITCHED AWAY FROM...

                      FOR MONSTER GO GO... FROM THE

                      LEFT BANK OF THE HUDSON RIVER! 2"

                  CUE : THE LIVE BAND

:12

     COMMERCIAL   ANGELO TV   LEAD IN TO: JOB CORPS (TO BLACK :15

FOLLOWS COMMERCIAL

LEAD OUT   JOB CORPS

INTRO   WM BONNIE

BARRY:

NUMBERS ON BACK OF
MALE PARTNERS FOR
CONTEST AFTER LIP SINC

(THE LEFT BANK
TO BE JUDGES)

COUPLES
READY

HE LIP SINCS THE ET

ET "........................"

(PICK UP THE DANCING)

ZACK GETS IN THE BOX (CANT STAND
LIP SINCS)

SEG TC "WOLFCALL"

:16   ZACK OUT OF THE BOX

".... TIME FOR THE MONSTER

REM

GO GO CONTEST...

BAND

ZACK RUNS TO STAGE WITH THE BAND MEMBERS   ALL NON CONTETANTS

CLEAR FLOOR TO BEHIND CAME
CAMERAS

8 COUPLES   JUDGES PICK FOUR BEST TO STAY

ET "CARA LIN" 2 32

OPEN MIKES FOR JUDGES CONFLAB

(PICK UP SHOTS OF TIRED DANCERS) FAST DECISSIONEI   FOUR COUPLES LEFT

ET "GOOD LOVIN" 2 28

OPEN MIKES

TIRED COUPLES   FAST DECISSION   TWO COUPLES LEFT

ET "NEW ORLEANS" 2 50

CONTESTANTS
BACK

:26

WINNER   GTEETS THE PRIZE

BOY HAS TO CLIMB INTO THE BAG FOR
PRIZE...   (OVER) CONTIUED NEXT PAGE   YEAH!

BOY IN THE BAG... OUT WITH THE PRIZES

BACK IN AGAIN...

ZACK PULLS THE DRAW STRING TIGHT   AND

DANCES WITH HIS GIRL

TO : ET "WHAT THE WORLD NEEDS NOW " 3 :10

contestants DANCING   AT START FOR MINUTE

OTHER GUESTS JOIN IN THEN

LET THE BOY OUT OF THEBAG

COMMERCIAL   LEAD IN TO FISCHER THE BREAD...   (LEFT BANK GET SET)

:31

INTRO THE LEFT BANK..

:37

ZAXK GATHER THE GANG FROM GRIGGSTOWN

FOR A SPECIAL IN THE CAVE...

TC "THE WORD" 2 42

SEG ET "DAYDREAM" 2 18

:42   COMMERCIAL BREAK   LEAD IN TO PHSYCAL FITNESS   (TO BLACK :15)

SEG OUT OF BLACK :   ET "CALIFORNIA DREAMIN"
2 :37

DURING CALIFORNIA DREAMIN   BAND GET SET TO

HOP ON STAGE.

THANKS FOR THE PRE SHOW PICNIC TO :

BACKCTOMCHEMLECTCBANK

PROMO MARCH 6

MENTION THEM ALL

LAST ON THE LIST...

"   THE LEFT BANK!"

CUE   LIVE BAND

FACE
CAVE   CU MAGUIRE   LIP SINGS THE OPENING INTRO ON   ET
GBGMCMBROMCECMEMEMSBCMCMCHHHM

ET "LATIN LUPE LU" 2 59

TC "UP TIGHT" 2 53

ET "LIKE A BABY" 2 54

ET "19th NERVOUS BREAKDOWN" 3 50

Dear Joette —

Sunday

I hate this sort of thing — but —

since Disc-O-Teen —

Radio — WRFM-FM about 4 yrs.

WPLJ about 9 years.

(I'M GUESSING!!)

then I officially gave it all up for whatever free-lance work came my way and found life to be really fine — not having to show up on time each day at some work place no matter how pleasant the work and fellow-workers might have been!

so since then I've poked around in my convert. — travelled to California to visit a certain lady — had bit parts ("Cameos," they call them) in a couple of scarey movies — and two videos "Nosferatu" or "Famous Monsters" — and lately I've become a sort of Mr. Nostalgia at Conventions — and that has been great fun; meeting people who recall the old days of TV and radio.

But the best fun of all will be the Feb. 3 re-union — that will become the All-time memory for me; I'm counting the days.

Zach.

A letter from Zach to Joette Hampton-Martin, a Disc-O-Teen dancer, on the eve of a 1991 Disc-O-Teen reunion. In it, Zach writes about his work in the quarter-century since the show went off the air.

7

PHOTO GHOULLERY

DOZENS OF ADDITIONAL PHOTOS OF JOHN ZACHERLE, PLUS OTHER RELATED MATERIAL, FROM HIS ROLAND DAYS TO HIS PRESENT DAZE

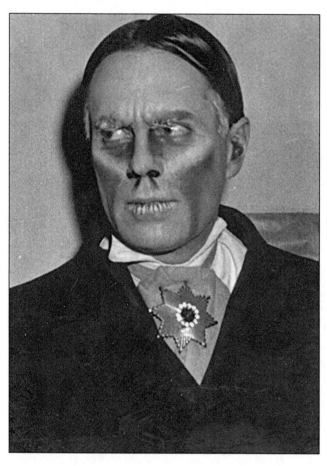

ZACH: *"At WCAU, they [his bosses] first decided that I should look like my lips had been sewn together — like a shrunken head. But they gave it up after about a week. They didn't think it looked good. Nobody could remember offhand what Bela Lugosi looked like but they thought I should look like him. As Dracula, he slicked his hair straight back so I don't know why we parted mine in the middle. Otherwise it was just overhead lighting making shadows on my cheeks and all that stuff. In black-and-white, people didn't get very clear pictures anywhere, except maybe in the control room. So the makeup kind of blurred a little bit."*

If you can find one of these fan club cards with the words "Blue Bell Studios" printed on the reverse side (instead of the words "Printed in the Moonlight by Little Bats in Transylvania"), you've got something rare!

Fan Club #........................

President

....

Printed in the Moonlight
by Little Bats
In Transylvania

Be it known to all that

....

is an Honored Member of
the Royal Order of the Un-
Dead Creatures of Darkness,
and as such is duty bound to
howl at The Full Moon when
in the presence of another
card-carrying member!

John Zacherle

Twelve-year-old fan Rosemary Schroeder did her homework after watching one of Zach's "lectures," drawing and sending him this piece of art.

On the next (many) pages are photos of Zach hosting (and behind the scenes) on Disc-O-Teen. *Here he is clowning with Barry Landers, the show's creator and co-executive producer.*

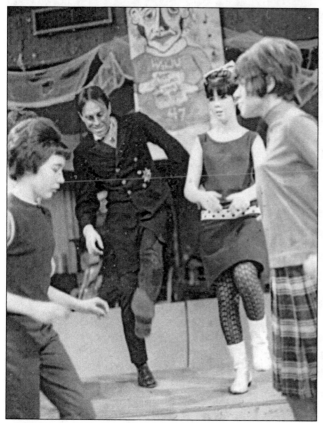

Zacherley on a "costume" episode of Disc-O-Teen, *sporting his "Italian fruit vendor" look.*

The late makeup man Michael R. Thomas makes one of his Disc-O-Teen *appearances.*

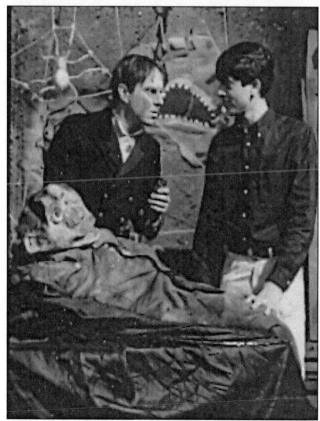

The girl in the middle is Joette Martin, recipient of the Zach letter found on page 195. Incidentally...why a duck?

An ad promoting Zach during his 1970s rock deejay days.

RIGHT: *Zach with a VHS copy of* Horrible Horror *(1986), in which he did his inimitable 1950s-60s horror host act.*

Zach with Famous Monsters *publisher Ray Ferry and editor Forry Ackerman.*

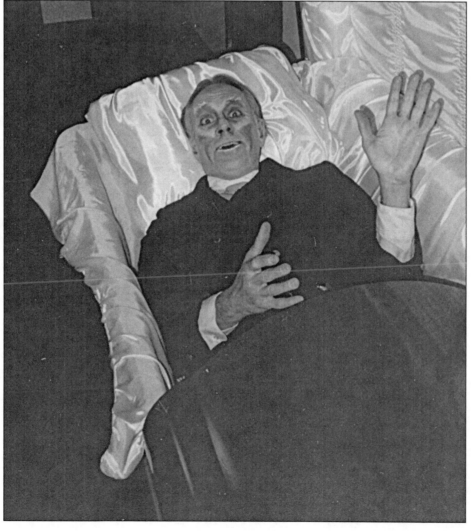

HENRY WINKLER

Zach—

Loud thank yous—
The note and tape
are so appreciated.

I know its a little
early, but . . .

Happy The beginning.

I can't wait to
watch the tape—

Warmly,

Henry W.

Oct 27th 2005

March 22, 2005

I can't tell you, John, how much I appreciate your stream of magnificent dialogue filled with memories and good wishes. The DVD was remarkable! You are truly outstanding and amazing.

I can't tell you how much your words meant to me. I assumed your DVD was some promotional tool for an upcoming production. Little did I realize, it was so personalized and intimate.

My best wishes to you, "The Cool Ghoul". May you reign supreme for many more years!

Sincerely,

Dick

Dick Clark

DC/as

Mr. John Zacherle
125 W. 96th Street
Apt. 4B
New York, NY 10025-6423

dick clark productions, inc.

*For his 90th birthday, Zach received congratulatory letters
from the mayors of New York City (Mike Bloomberg) and
Newark (Cory A. Booker).*

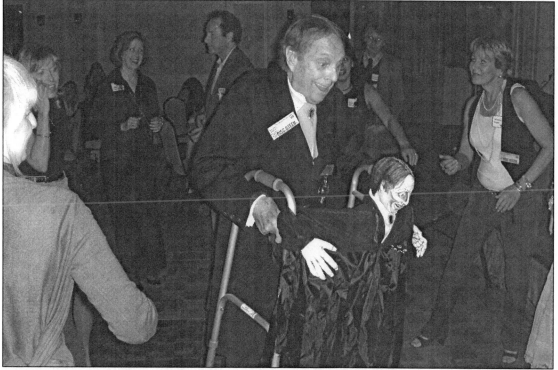

ABOVE: *In 2007, Zach is flanked by* Disc-O-Teen *alumni Christine Domaniecki, Michael R. Thomas, Rich Scrivani and Marsha Silvestri on the street outside Newark NJ's Mosque Theater where the show originated.* BELOW: *At the second* Disc-O-Teen *reunion (2007), a nearly-90 Zach horses around with a walker made for him by diehard fan Rosemary Schroeder DiPietra.*

Zach's 90th birthday gift from Miami fan Sharon Shaw: a permanent lakeside bench with plaque in Harriman Park, New York. Notice Zach's reflected image in the plaque.

On September 22, 2008, 50 years to the day after making his WABC-TV debut, Zacherley poses with a picture of himself and a copy of the 1958 TV Guide *listing that first* Shock Theater *appearance. The movie that historic night in 1958 was* Mystery of Edwin Drood *(1935).*

Whenever a Shock Theater *called for Zach to sing, his coffin-bound off-camera wife was supposedly accompanying on piano — but it was actually played by Earl Wild (1915-2010) in the lean years before he achieved fame as a world-class pianist. In 2008, the two reunited backstage at Carnegie Hall after a Wild performance.*

When he saw this photo for the first time, Zach said he wished there'd been this type of lighting on Shock Theater.

ABOVE: *Zach and New York airwave legend "Cousin Brucie" (Bruce Morrow) in 2010.* BELOW: *Beauties and the Beast!*

TV HORROR-HOSTING FIRST BROUGHT JOHN ZACHERLE TO PROMINENCE IN THE 1950S AND '60S. IN THE 1990S AND 2000S, THE "SECOND COMING" OF ZACH WAS THANKS TO THE "CHILLER THEATRE" EXPOS AND THEIR ORGANIZER KEVIN CLEMENT (PICTURED BELOW, WITH ZACH). AT THESE CROWDED NEW JERSEY CONVENTIONS, ZACH HAS MET AND SIGNED AUTOGRAPHS FOR THOUSANDS OF LONGTIME FANS AND MADE THOUSANDS OF NEW ONES.

RIGHT: *Zach BFF Jeff Samuels helps him at every Chiller.*

BELOW: *Ray Manzarek, keyboard player for The Doors, pays his respects to fellow Chiller guest Zach. Decades earlier, Manzarek and the other Doors appeared on* Disc-O-Teen.

ABOVE: *Zach and adult film star Marilyn Chambers at Chiller.* BELOW: *Zach's friend Arnie DeGaetano (bearded) presents him with a new undertaker's coat. Zach CD producer and back-up musician Mike Gilks is on the left, Mike's wife Ruth on the right.*

AFTERWORD

Zacherley! To me, the name summons up childhood memories of countless nights in front of my television set getting my first real education on horror films and macabre humor! Then, on *Disc-O-Teen*, he re-emerged as the coolest Transylvanian rock & roll host on my UHF converter box with some great bands of the day!

I would never have imagined that this Cool Ghoul would become my friend almost two and a half decades later: When I decided to start putting on a convention, he was my first choice to kick it off and be my first guest! It was a great experience that continues to this day. In 21 years putting on the Chiller Theatre Expo, Zach has been there for every single show!! Broken foot or whatever, he has been there!

Zach once told me something that I will always cherish: He said that being at the Chiller Theatre Expo every six months is like tana leaves to the Mummy — it recharges his batteries! I think it's really the opposite: I think Zach appearing every six months at Chiller Theatre really recharges all of our batteries and restores a part of our lost youth.

He is one of the nicest persons I have ever met in my life and I love him like a father, a brother, a friend...there will never be another like the one and only John Zacherle. I will never forget his generosity and graciousness over the decades to me and the fans who have come to see the undisputed King of TV Horror Hosts!!

Kevin Clement
Chiller Theatre
April 2012

Secret revealed: How a Cool Ghoul stays cool!

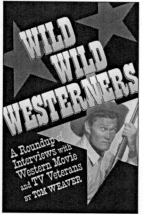

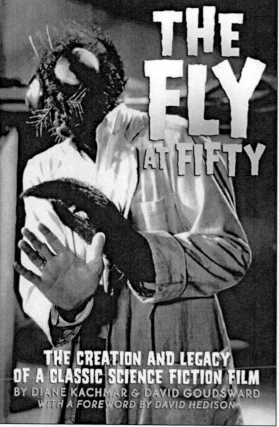
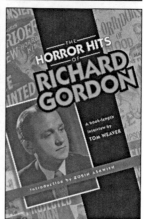

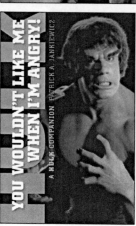

CPSIA information can be obtained at www.ICGtesting.com
Printed in the USA
LVOW071156070712

288963LV00002B/76/P